Scrap-O-LATOR

QUILTS & MORE

dianne springer

 American Quilter's Society
P. O. Box 3290 • Paducah, KY 42002-3290
www.AmericanQuilter.com

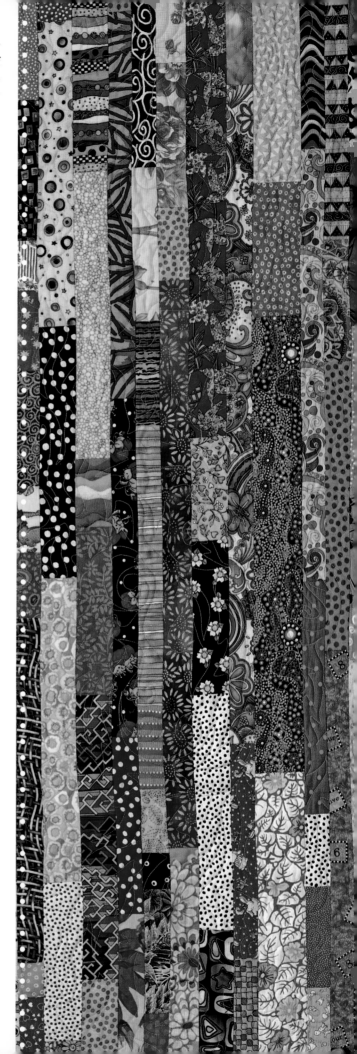

Located in Paducah, Kentucky, the American Quilter's Society (AQS) is dedicated to promoting the accomplishments of today's quilters. Through its publications and events, AQS strives to honor today's quiltmakers and their work and to inspire future creativity and innovation in quiltmaking.

EXECUTIVE BOOK EDITOR: ANDI MILAM REYNOLDS
COPY EDITOR: BARBARA PITMAN
GRAPHIC DESIGN: MELISSA POTTERBAUM
COVER DESIGN: MICHAEL BUCKINGHAM
PHOTOGRAPHY: CHARLES R. LYNCH
ADDITIONAL PHOTOGRAPHY: THOMAS SPRINGER
ILLUSTRATIONS, PAGES 6, 19, 22, 27-28, 31, 46-48, 55, 62, 74: DIANNE SPRINGER

Additional copies of this book may be ordered from the American Quilter's Society, PO Box 3290, Paducah, KY 42002-3290, or online at www.AmericanQuilter.com.

Text © 2012, Author, Dianne Springer
Artwork © 2012, American Quilter's Society

American Quilter's Society
P. O. Box 3290 • Paducah, KY 42002-3290
www.AmericanQuilter.com

LIBRARY OF CONGRESS CATALOGING-IN-PUBLICATION DATA

Springer, Dianne (Dianne E.), 1945-
  Scrap-o-lator quilts & more / by Dianne Springer.
    p. cm.
  Summary: "Make 13 projects using fabric scraps"--Provided by publisher.
  ISBN 978-1-60460-015-5
  1. Patchwork--Patterns. 2. Patchwork quilts. I. Title. II. Title: Scrap-o-lator quilts and more.
  TT835.S654 2012
  746.46--dc23
             2011040916

DEDICATION

How does one go about thanking those who surround them with love, support, encouragement, and anything else that is needed? There really are no words adequate enough to express my appreciation to each and every one of them.

There have been so many who have shared my work, inspired me, and helped me, but I will name just Hannah Marie Lee of Choudrant, Louisiana. She has been my friend, mentor, and teacher from the very beginning of my quilting adventures. She deserves much of the credit (or should I say blame?) for my introduction into the world of quilting. For everything it has added to my life, Hannah, I thank you.

I dedicate this book to Tom, my amazing "Mr. Wonderful" for lo these many years, and to my daughter, Brandy, who works harder than anyone I know. I love you both with all my heart.

IN MEMORY

In memory of my wonderful sister, and best friend, Debbie, who loved having fun and supported every nutty idea I have had. The memories of our Roman trip make me laugh to this day. I will miss you every day for the rest of my life.

Deborah Lee Emery
January 24, 1951 – November 17, 2011

TITLE PAGE: TABLE SCRAPS, detail. Full project on page 33.
THIS PAGE AND OPPOSITE: SCRAP-O-LATOR II, detail. Full quilt on page 13.

TABLE OF CONTENTS

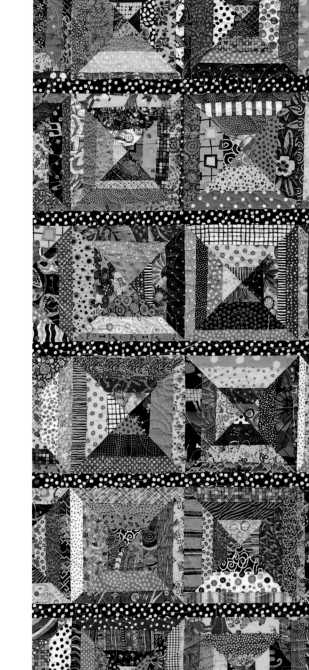

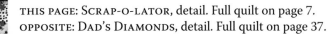

THIS PAGE: Scrap-o-lator, detail. Full quilt on page 7.
OPPOSITE: Dad's Diamonds, detail. Full quilt on page 37.

PREFACE

A hooker.

I have aspired to be one ever since I heard about them. No, it has nothing to do with drugs, fortunately, and nothing to do with sex, unfortunately.

I first heard this word used in connection with education many years ago. It is when a university department has its best professors teaching freshman classes. The plan is for the students to be so inspired that they major in that field, thus increasing that department's enrollment, status, funding, and bragging rights. It works. A local university chemistry professor lectured in my son's fifth grade class and hooked my son on science.

If you are not already hooked on quilting, I want to be your hooker. Of course, I am delighted when I hook anyone on anything that excites me. I taught in a talented visual arts program for 25 years and did my level best to hook as many students on art as I possibly could. If enthusiasm is the key, I am your man, uh, woman, whatever.

One has to assume that you are already at least interested in quilting or crafts or you would not even have read this far. Since I have difficulty focusing on any one medium, this book is not "all about quilting." I have included projects for people who don't sew, as well. My main goal is having FUN. After many years of marriage, it seems that the philosophy of my incredible husband, who lives by the hedonistic belief that "pleasure is good," has finally rubbed off on me. I hope it rubs off on you, and you, too, get hooked.

If you have only made one quilt or ever sewn at all, you have scraps—the more quilts, the more scraps, and the larger your stash. This book is all about scraps and making creative use of them. I also favor "functional." So, whenever possible, the objects we are making are not just pretty, but can be useful, too. Thus, the name of my book— *Scrap-o-Lator Quilts & More*. This should lessen your stash, ergo, making room for more, of course.

This book is divided into two parts. The first part is mainly quilts, certainly projects that relate to quilts and require sewing. The second part is devoted to projects that involve no sewing whatsoever.

From the outset, quilting seemed like a peculiar hobby to me. I mean, one would purchase a perfectly good piece of flat, rectangular fabric, then cut it up into tiny pieces, then sew it back together, ending up with a perfectly good piece of flat, rectangular fabric. Then I remembered that this was more of the "modern" approach to quilting. For so long, quilts were made of rescued items such as old shirts, pants, flour sacks, etc.—recycling at its best. Either way, I love the connection with the past.

By the time I had been quilting for two years, not only had I made about 80 quilts using that "modern" approach, I had accumulated two huge baskets of scraps. In order to save myself from having to purchase yet another huge basket for more scraps, I decided to eliminate my pile by making a huge quilt using nothing but what I had available. I had an art instructor who loved to say to his students, "You have what you need." I wanted to test that theory. My second goal: Buy nothing when piecing the top.

Thus, the beginning of the first quilt in this book, the one that would eliminate my scrap pile!

SEWING PROJECTS

Yardage for the Curious

For the curious—and we all know what curiosity did for that cat—it takes approximately three yards of cotton fabric to equal one pound. That might help when calculating your supplies for some of these quilts. Scraps are easier to measure by weight than by area.

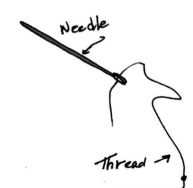

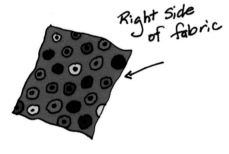

← wrong side of fabric

Right Side of fabric

My Take on General Directions

Somewhere about this page is where many books on quilting seem to feel the need to do what I consider to be reinventing the wheel. I mean, this is the place where great descriptions unfold on basic terms such as what is meant by a ¼" seam, how to press that seam, how to make a binding, etc.

It is my belief that this information is not necessary in a book based on the premise that you, the reader, have a pre-existing stash of fabric caused by a pre-existing knowledge of and love for sewing.

So, except for this commentary, this part of this book is unwritten. If you feel the need for information, basic or otherwise, my number is (318) 247-9725. Actually, I love to talk about just about anything, so feel free to call me if you have the inclination.

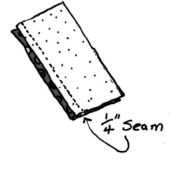

¼" Seam

Scissors →

Needle

Thread →

SCRAP-O-LATOR
A.K.A. The Plan to Eliminate My Scraps

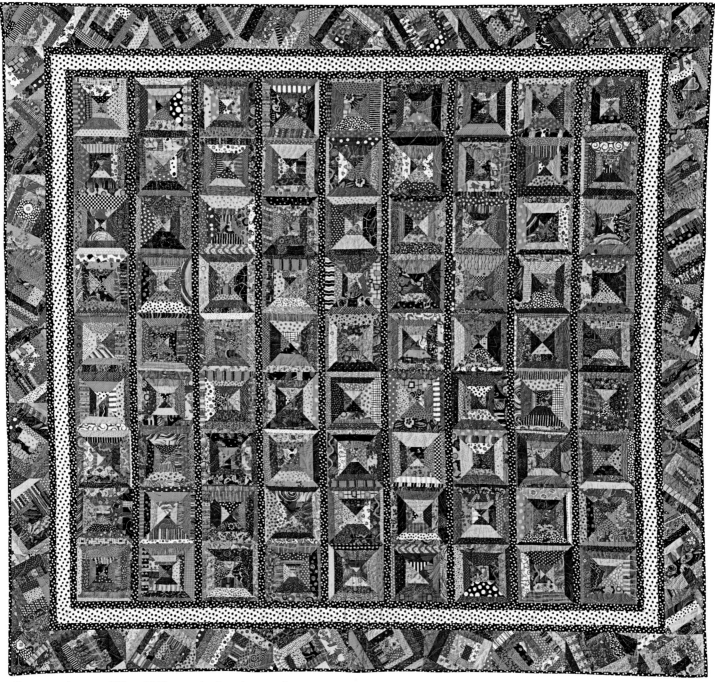

SCRAP-O-LATOR, 92" x 100", made by the author

In addition to setting a goal to not purchase any new fabric for this quilt, I also wanted to keep decision-making to a minimum. I did not worry about the length or width of my scraps, the color, the fabric patterns, or much of anything else, for that matter.

I tried not to judge each fabric, but simply chose each piece randomly. This is pretty much a worry-free quilt with very little matching of anything. As you can see, I love polka dots, so I used them as a repeating element in this design. And, no, I did not cheat. These fabrics were the trimmings from an earlier quilt.

Notes

- First and foremost, please make yourself read through all directions before proceeding with the really fun part of the process.
- Assume all seams are the standard ¼".
- Press seams toward the bottom on all the quarter-square triangles.
- For me, "scrap" means a piece of fabric too small to worry about folding (a.k.a. stuff that you would have thrown away before you learned about quilting). "Stash" is closer to "yardage."

Materials

Quilt top: Lots and lots of scraps, the equivalent of about 8 yards of fabric (about 2⅔ pounds). The pieces need to have at least two straight, parallel edges but can be any length or width. You can sew different scraps together; just be sure to trim them to the same width, such as 2½" or 1¾", etc.

Black/white polka dot sashing, inner borders, and binding: 2½ yards
Sashing:
- 10 strips, 72½" x 1½"
- 2 strips, 82½" x 1½"
- 2 strips, 78½" x 1½"
- 2 strips, 88½" x 1½"

Binding:
- 5 strips, 2½" x length of fabric (2½ yards)

White/black polka dot inner border: 1 yard
- 2 strips, 74½" x 2½"
- 2 strips, 86½" x 2½"

Batting:
- "Generous queen," 100" x 108"

Backing:
- 7½ yards

Outside border: Lightweight foundation
Material:
- 36 pieces, cut 11" x 7"

Other things:
- Triangular template (quarter-square) that measures at least 4½" from top to bottom, down the middle
- Steam-A-Steam®

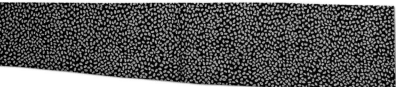

Figure 1

Top and Inner Borders

1. Begin by randomly selecting a piece of fabric (it helps to close your eyes). It should have at least one straight side. Sew the straight side to a second, slightly longer piece, with the longer edges and right sides together. I am already at this point thinking of a triangular shape so the next piece I attach should be longer than the first two (figure 1).

2. Do not worry if some pieces are short. Simply sew them together to get longer ones. Then, trim them to the same width. When you have at least 5" of strips sewn together (that's measuring from the top edge of the first strip to the bottom edge of the last strip) (figure 2), trim to a quarter square that is at least 4½" from top to bottom of the triangle (figure 3).

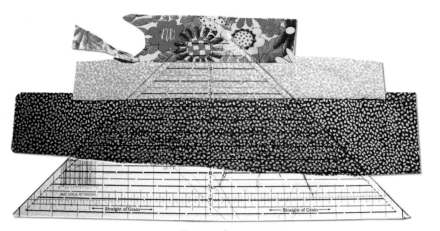

Figure 2

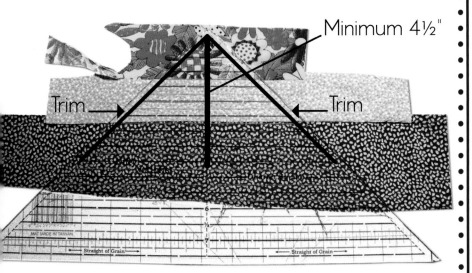

Minimum 4½"

Trim →   ← Trim

Figure 3

3. Repeat step 1 until you have enough to make 81 complete squares (81 x 4 = 324 quarters).

4. With right sides together, sew two quarters together along one edge, starting at the top "point" of the triangle (figure 4).

5. Repeat with two more quarters. Sew the two half squares together (figure 5), matching seams at the points of the triangles. The points are the only places you need to be concerned about "matching." Continue making squares until you have 81 completed ones.

6. Trim the squares to 8½" x 8½".

Figure 4

Figure 5

Figure 6

7. Join 9 squares together in a row (figure 6). Set aside.

8. Repeat step 7 until you have a total of 9 rows.

9. Sew one 72½" x 1½" black/white polka dot strip to one of the long edges of a row of 9. Sew another 72½" x 1½" polka-dotted strip to the other long edge of the same row of 9 (figure 7).

10. Add another row of the 9 squares from step 8. Continue alternately adding a row of 9, then a polka-dot strip as shown in figure 7 until you have used all 9 rows of squares.

11. End by adding the last 72½" x 1½" polka-dotted strip.

12. Using the 82½" x 1½" black/white polka dotted strips, sew them to the remaining edges of the quilt.

13. Next, add the white-with-black polka dots border pieces, 74½" x 2½", to both ends of the quilt. Then add the 86½" x 2½" border strips to the outside edges.

14. Sew a 78½" x 1½" strip of the black/white polka dots to the top and bottom edges of the quilt. Then, add the remaining 88½" x 1½" black/white dotted strips to the outer edges of the quilt top. Set the quilt top aside at this point.

Figure 7

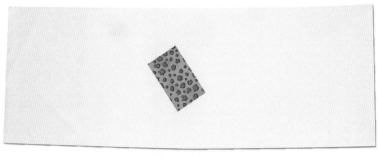

Outside Border

1. Place a square or rectangular scrap right-side up at an angle to the edges of one of the foundation pieces in the approximate middle of the foundation piece (figure 8). This small rectangle or square should be no larger than, say, 3" x 3". Again, it is not terribly critical. Add a second scrap to the first by placing it right-sides together, longer edges aligned. Sew through all thicknesses. Flip so the right sides are up and press. Turn the foundation piece 90 degrees and add a third strip. Sew. Trim excess fabric from underneath the scrappy strips so it will not get too bulky. Flip open, press (figure 9).

Figure 8

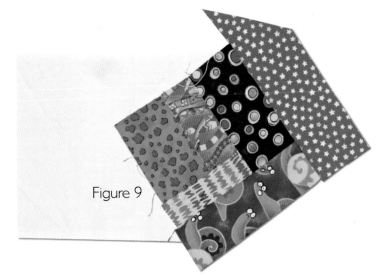

Figure 9

2. Continue adding scraps until the foundation piece is covered (figure 10). Trim to 10½" x 6½". Set aside.

3. Complete all 36 pieces of foundation fabric in the same manner as the first. Trim all to the 10½" x 6½" size.

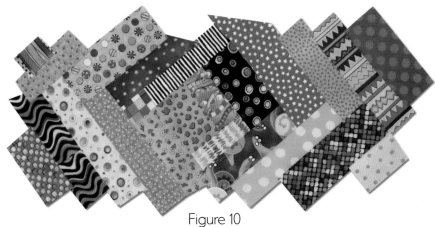

Figure 10

4. Sew 8 of these pieces together, end to end (6½" to the 6½" edges). Add this strip of 8 to one end of the quilt.

5. Repeat step 4 with 8 more completed foundation pieces. Add this strip of 8 to the opposite side of the quilt.

6. Now sew 10 completed foundation pieces together. Sew this strip to the outer side of the quilt.

7. Repeat with the remaining 10 foundation pieces. Add this strip to the last edge of the quilt. Sandwich the quilt top/batting/backing, then quilt in your favorite design. Trim.

Binding

1. Sew the 5 strips 2" x 90" of black/white polka dots together. Add a small strip of Steam-A-Seam 2® to the right side of one end. Do not remove the paper at this time. Turn under about ¼" so the Steam-A-Seam 2 is to the inside. Press the strip in half lengthwise.

2. Place the long raw edges of the binding along the raw edges of the right side of the quilt. Begin sewing about 3" from the Steam-A-Seam 2 end.

3. When you are about 2" or 3" from going all the way around, stop and trim the binding so it overlaps the beginning edge by about 1".

4. Remove the adhesive paper and place the end piece inside the turned Steam-A-Seam 2 edge. Press and complete the stitching.

5. Turn the binding to the back and hand stitch to cover the raw edges of the quilt.

Ta-da! It's a quilt.

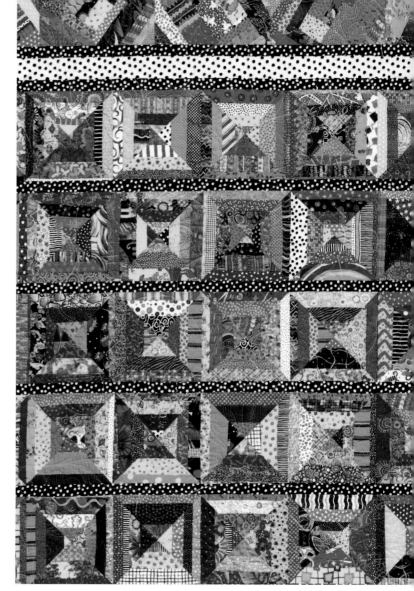

SCRAP-O-LATOR II

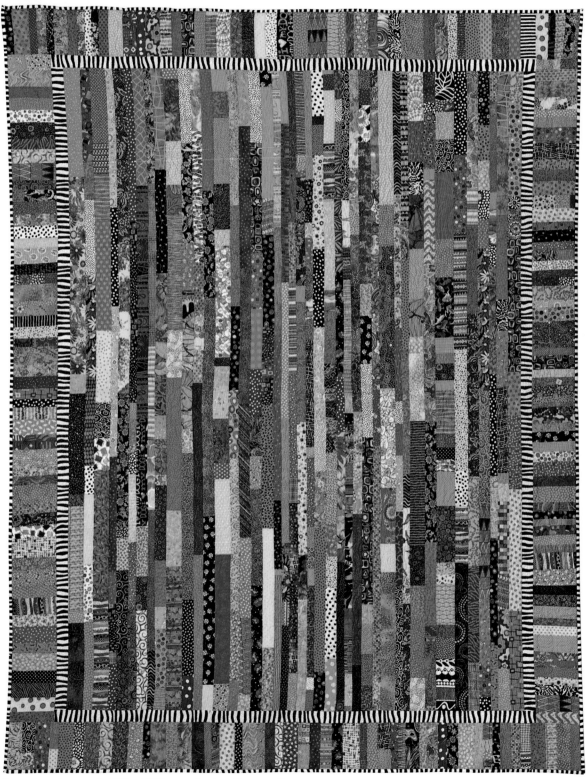

SCRAP-O-LATOR II, 72" x 92", made by the author

As I mentioned earlier, when I began the first of what ended up being a series of quilt projects, my goal was to "terminate" my basket of scraps. To be honest, I had two very large baskets of scraps. At the risk of repeating myself, my self-imposed challenge had two parts: first, to not buy any fabric whatsoever for the piecing of the quilt; and second, to eliminate the scrap stash as much as possible. I am delighted to say that I met part one of my challenge for SCRAP-O-LATOR. I succeeded in completing the top without buying one teensy-weensy new piece of fabric.

As for the second phase of the challenge, the only thing that seemed to have changed about my large supply of scraps was that I no longer needed a compactor to keep it contained. Thus, The SCRAP-O-LATOR II, and SCRAP-O-LAP, and, well, enough projects to fill a book.

So, again, this quilt is all about scraps and stashes and their transformation into a wonderful, fun quilt. You do not need to concern yourself with matching your colors, matching fabric designs, or with matching most of the seams. Let the second party begin!

Notes
- Press all seams in the same direction.
- All seams are ¼".

Materials

Quilt top: Lots of scraps, about the equivalent of 7 or 8 yards of fabric (about 2 or 2½ pounds)

Inner border: ½ yard total, pieced to become 2 strips 60½" x 2" and 2 strips 77½" x 2"

Outer border: 5 strips you will cut from the completed quilt top (really)

Backing: 6 yards of 40" fabric

Batting: 80" x 100" (or 90" x 108", which is queen size, mostly, because that is the size I buy all the time)

Binding: ¾ yard total (whether scraps or stash, a.k.a., one fabric, you will piece/cut 9 strips 2½" x width of fabric)

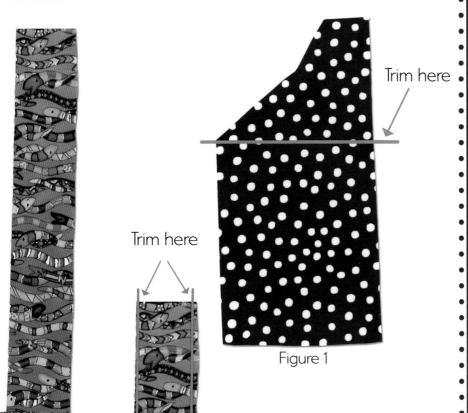

Trim here

Trim here

Figure 1

Figure 2

Figure 3

Figure 4

Quilt Top

1. To make this easy, I grouped my scraps into three width piles: narrow, medium, and wide. The only cutting to be done at this point is to trim any piece that does not have two straight, parallel ends (figure 1).

2. Sew pieces from the narrowest width pile end to end until you get a strip at least 112" long (figure 2).

3. Trim these pieces so that the width is the same the entire length of each strip (figure 3). In other words, you will be trimming down to the narrowest piece in the strip (therein lies the *raison d'etre* for the grouping of the fabrics—less waste). Continue making strips until the pile is gone.

4. Do the same thing with the other two piles of fabric.

5. Mix the piles of strips into one large pile. Randomly select two strips from the pile and then sew these two strips together along the long edges (figure 4).

6. Continue adding strips as in (figure 5) until your quilt top is 62" wide.

7. Straighten up the top and bottom edges. Now, to make the outer border, cut 5 strips off the quilt top, side to side, 6½" x 62" (figure 6). Set them aside. Square up the remaining quilt top to 57½" x 77½".

Inner Border

1. Using the 77½" x 2" inner border strips, sew 1 to each of the longer sides of the quilt top. Now, add the 60½" x 2" inner border strips to the top and bottom edges.

Outer Border

1. Trim 2 of the 6½" x 62" strips cut from the top to 60½" (6½" x 60½") and then sew them to the top and bottom edges of the quilt.

2. Cut 1 of the 3 remaining strips in half (6½" x 31").

3. Sew 1 of these halves to one of the remaining 62" pieces (6½" x 93"). Trim to 92½" wide and then sew this to 1 of the outer sides of the quilt. Repeat for the other side.

Figure 5

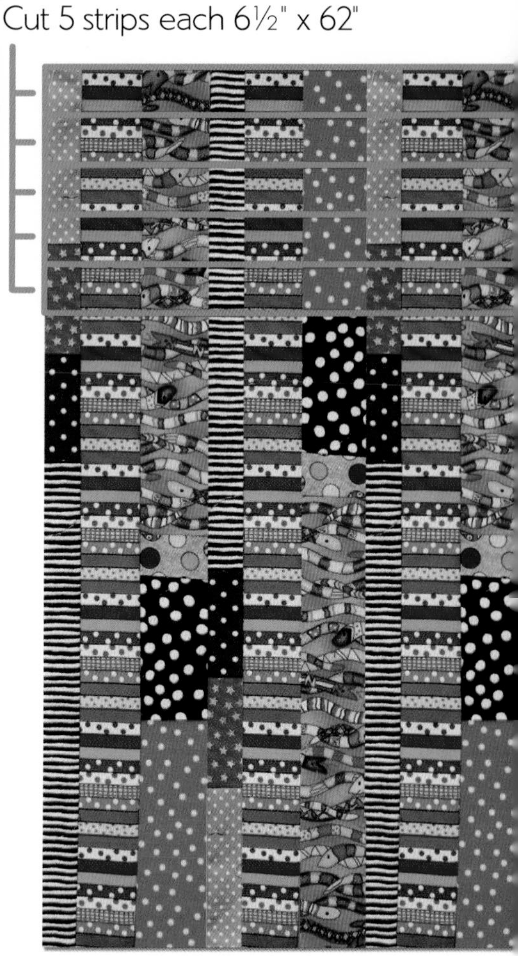

Cut 5 strips each 6½" x 62"

Figure 6

Backing

1. Cut 6 yards (216") of 40" fabric into two 3-yard pieces (figure 7).

2. Trim selvages. Sew the pieces together along the 3-yard edges to get an 80" x 108" piece (figure 8, page 17).

Backing 6 yards (216") x 40"

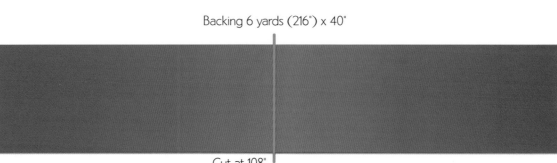

Cut at 108"

Figure 7

Backing 80" x 108"

Seam

Figure 8

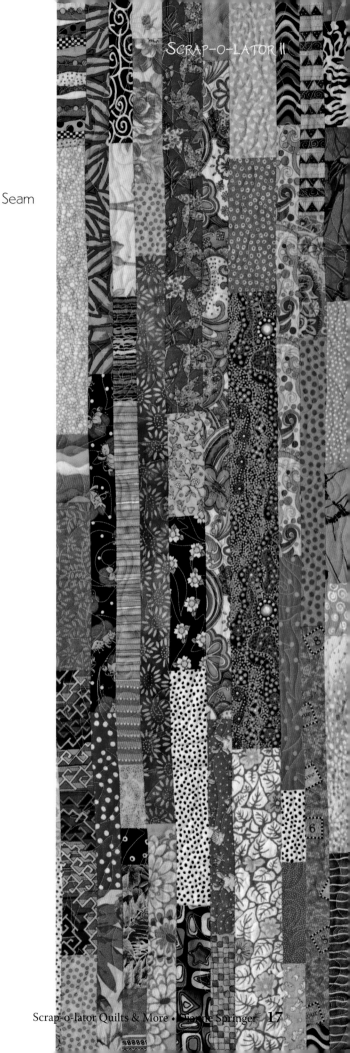

3. Sandwich top/batting/backing. Get this baby to the quilting machine, quickly. I cannot wait to see it finished, so run to the nearest place, get it quilted, and bind, bind, bind.

Binding

1. You will need a binding strip of at least 350" x 2½". You may achieve this by using yardage, in which case you simply need to cut 9 strips 2½" wide x the width of the fabric. Sew these together to get a piece 360" long. Press in half, stitch, turn, sew, yada, yada, yada (see page 12 if you don't understand "yada").

2. If you are using scraps, cut pieces 2½" wide x whatever length is available. Sew these together until the strip is at least 350" long. More yada, yada, yada (again, see page 12 if you don't understand "yada").

3. Finally, take pictures and send them to me! I would love to add them to my blog, Threads from My Head (www.diannespringer. com). While you are playing on the computer and not quilting, be sure to check out www. MyQuiltPlace.com for even more fun!

SCRAP-O-LAP QUILT

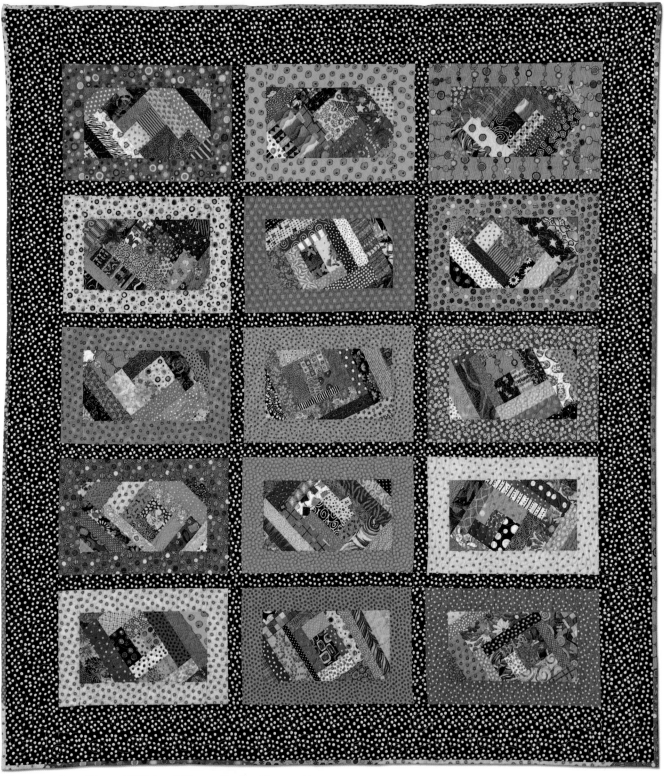

SCRAP-O-LAP QUILT, 57½" x 65", made by the author

One might jump to the conclusion that because this baby is a much smaller quilt than either of the first two that I am finally running out of scraps. So NOT happening. This quilt was actually the result of a suggestion from my husband. He said, "Honey, not everyone needs such large quilts. Why don't you make a smaller one this time?" So, totally out of character for me, I took his advice. He is still in shock...

One other thing different about this quilt, other than its size, is the part where I actually dipped into my stash (yardage) for some of the borders. But, I am still within my goals—no purchasing, so far. I even had enough for the backing. Whoopee.

Notes
• Be sure to read through all instructions before assembling.
• This is a "do as I say, not as I do" kind of thing, but, for the record, you have been advised.
• All seams are ¼".

Materials

Lightweight foundation fabric: 1 yard cut into 15 pieces 7" x 12" (white muslin works well)

Scraps: approximately 1½ yards of scraps of various sizes (about ½ pound)

Sashing: 15 different fabrics—red, orange, yellow, turquoise, blue, green, pink—each at least 12" x 12". Cut each fabric into 2 strips 2½" x 10½" and 2 strips 2½" x 11½".

Inner and outer borders: Black/white polka dot (total of 2 yards, about ⅔ pound) (w/ pieced outer border, 1½ yards).

Cut the border fabric into 10 strips 1¾" x 10½" and 4 strips 1¾" x 48" plus 2 strips 5½" x 48" and 2 strips 5½" x 65½". See Polka Dot Cutting Diagram.

Backing: 3 yards

Batting: 60" x 70"

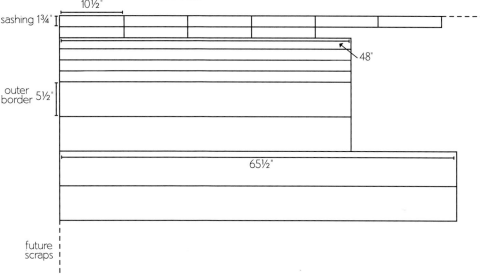

Polka Dot Cutting Diagram

Quilt Top

1. Using 1 of the pieces of foundation fabric and fabric from the scrap pile, begin by placing 1 small scrappy piece (approximately 2" x 3", not critical, it just needs to be a small rectangle or square) face up on the foundation fabric. The small piece of fabric should be placed in the approximate center of the foundation fabric and its outer edges should be at an angle to the outside edges of the foundation piece (figure 1).

2. Using a second piece from the scrap pile, place it right-sides together on top of the first scrap, one of the longer edges aligned with one of the longer edges of the first piece. Stitch along this edge, open, press, and then trim any excess fabric from under the seam (figure 2).

3. Moving in a clockwise direction, add another scrap to the first two, right-sides together, stitch, open, press, trim (figure 3).

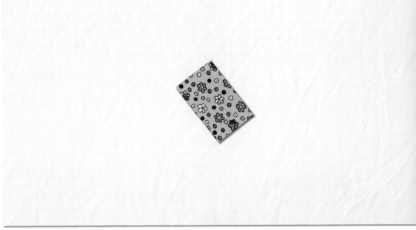

Figure 1

Figure 2

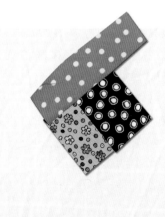

Figure 3

4. Continue adding scraps in this fashion until all of the foundation fabric is covered (figure 4).

5. Trim to a 6½" x 11½" rectangle (figure 5).

6. Repeat until all of the foundation pieces are covered and trimmed.

Sashing

1. Pick 1 of the sashing colors to add borders to 1 of the finished foundation pieces. Sew 1 of the 2½" x 11½" pieces to each of the longer sides of the foundation piece.

2. Next, add the shorter, 2½" x 10½" pieces to the sides of that same foundation piece (figure 6).

3. Complete each of the 15 finished foundation blocks with a different color sashing.

4. Lay the blocks out in a 3 x 5 configuration to determine the color placement. When you are satisfied with your design, sew them into rows in the order you have created. Alternate each foundation block with two of the 1¾" x 10½" strips of polka dot fabric, beginning and ending with the foundation blocks. Make five rows like this.

5. Sew a 1¾" x 48" strip of polka dot fabric to the bottom of one of these rows. Continue adding a row, then a strip, until you have used all of the rows and all of the 1¾" x 48" strips.

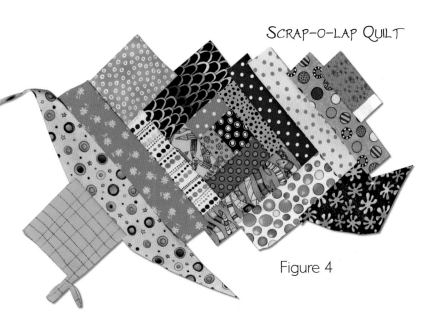

Figure 4

Figure 5

Figure 6

6. Add 1 of the 5½" x 48" border pieces to the top and 1 to the bottom of the quilt.

7. Finish the top by sewing the remaining 2 border pieces to the sides of the quilt.

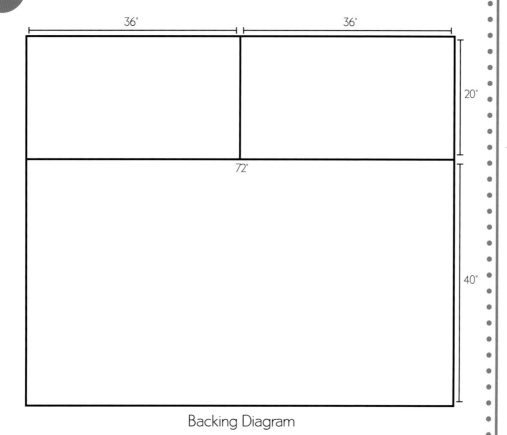

36"   36"

20"

72"

40"

Backing Diagram

Backing

1. See the diagram to sew the backing.

2. Cut 1 yard off the 3-yard piece. Cut this yard in half to make 2 pieces 36" x 20". Stitch these 2 pieces together along the 20" edges creating a 20" x 72" piece. Now sew the 2-yard strip and this new strip together along the 72" edges.

3. Sandwich top/batting/backing and quilt as desired. Trim to even the edges. You should end up with a 5" border.

Binding

1. In keeping with the idea that this is a scrappy quilt, I like to use a variety of scraps to make the binding. In this particular quilt, I used the leftover fabric from the 15 foundation blocks' sashing fabrics simply because I had enough. Do not worry if you do not have enough of those; just use what you have. It is a little more work, but to me, way worth it.

2. Cut pieces that are 2½" wide but that vary in length (approximately 12" to 24" long). You will need to create a strip at least 260" long. I would pay attention to the colors, making sure you do not end up with several of the same color next to each other.

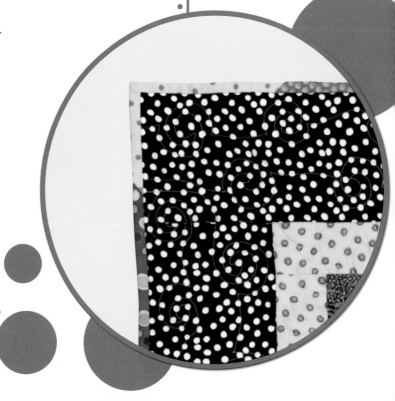

SCRAPPY REVERSIBLE PLACEMAT

Now we are really getting small. This in no way reflects the remainder of my stash. I still cannot see the bottom of the basket, even when I dig. Sigh.

At least I am having fun. Isn't that the point? Who can't use another set of placemats? Let's get started...

Scrappy Reversible Placemat (front), 13" x 20", made by the author

Scrappy Reversible Placemat (back), 13" x 20", made by the author

Notes

- Basically, the directions are for 1 reversible (two-sided) placemat but you can easily make placemats with only one appliquéd side.
- I press my seams in the same direction as I sew, either all to the left, or all to the right.
- All seams are ¼".

Materials

Background: A variety of black-and-white prints cut in various widths such as 1¼", 1½", 1¾", 2", 2¼", 2½", 2¾", etc., by whatever lengths you have available. Square off the ends. Total fabric needed is about 2 fat quarters for each side (about .4 pound).

Appliqués: A few scraps of yellow, blue, red, and green. You can sew pieces together to make them large enough to cut into the leaf shapes. Also, it would look great to use different colors for each of the petals on the flower.

Lightweight backing fabric for appliqués: ½ yard

Binding: ¼ yard. Make 2 strips cut 2½" x width of fabric sewn together to equal at least 2½" x 75"

when sewn together. I chose to use a black-and-white striped fabric simply because I had enough of it. Of course, you need to double this for 2 placemats.

Backing: Either use the second design to make the placemat reversible, or, use 1 fabric piece approximately 15" x 22" or scraps sewn together to equal that size for each placemat.

Bonding material: 2 yards of Steam-A-Seam 2 or Wonder-Under®

Batting: 15" x 22"

Great to have, but optional:
- tear-away stabilizer
- "sticky-fingered" gloves
- Teflon® sheet for machine quilting

Top Background

1. Begin by sewing strips of matching widths together, end-to-end to equal lengths that are at least 14" long (figure 1). For example, take one of the 2" wide strips and sew it to the end of another 2" wide piece. Some of your strips may already be long enough.

2. Now, start sewing these 14" length strips together lengthwise (figure 2).

3. Continue adding strips until the piece measures approximately 14" x 21".

4. To make the placemat reversible, repeat these steps to get a second piece the same size.

Figure 1

Figure 2

Preparing the Appliqués

1. Trace each of the appliqué designs on pages 27 & 28 onto the paper side of the bonding material. Cut out each design, leaving a small border. (Do not cut out on the lines at this point). Set aside.

2. Prepare each of the fabrics for each of the appliqué pieces thusly: For each appliqué part, cut 1 piece of backing and 1 piece of bonding material slightly larger than the appliqué design (for example, the leaf shape). Fuse the bonding material to the back of the backing fabric.

3. Remove the paper and fuse this backing to the wrong side of the appropriate fabric (for example, green for a leaf).

4. Now, bond the drawn leaf shape from step 1 to the back side of the bonded fabric. Cut out along the lines of the appliqué design. Remove the paper backing to expose the adhesive. (The easiest way is to lightly score the paper with a pin. It should remove easily. If it is too difficult to remove, stop and press again. Let cool completely before attempting to remove the paper.)

5. Repeat this procedure for each of the appliqué parts.

6. Place the appliqué pieces down on the placemat, starting with the stem (see page 26). Add the leaves, then the flower shapes. When you are satisfied with the placement, press carefully to adhere everything.

Figure 3

7. Now, take this placemat top and put it on top of a piece of batting. Use either the blanket stitch or a close zigzag stitch over the edges of all of the pieces. To make the smoothest transition on the curves, with the needle down, always rotate your fabric when the needle is to the outside of any curve, not the inside edge (figure 3).

8. If you are making a reversible placemat, repeat steps 3-6 with the second side. Place this second placemat on top of a sheet of tear-away stabilizer. Use either zigzag or blanket stitch over each appliqué shape. Remove the stabilizer.

9. Sandwich the two placemat tops, right-sides out. If you're making a single-sided placemat, use backing fabric. Using a stipple stitch or any other quilting technique, quilt the placemat.

10. Trim to approximately 13" x 20" doing most of the trimming on the sides and bottom. If you can get away with simply straightening the edges, do that. Making the placemat a little larger is not a problem.

Binding

1. Turn under ¼" on one of the binding strip ends and press. Add a small strip of Steam-A-Seam 2 to this turned edge. Do not remove the paper yet. Press the 2½" x 75" strip of binding in half lengthwise.

2. With the placemat right-side up, place the end with the Steam-A-Seam 2 on it first, matching long raw edges with the outside edges of the mat.

3. Start sewing about 2" or 3" from the beginning of the binding strip. Sew a generous ¼" seam through all thicknesses. When you get within 3" of the leading end, stop.

4. Trim the binding strip about 1" too long. Remove the paper from the beginning edge, exposing the adhesive from the Steam-A-Seam 2. Place the end piece inside this folded edge. Smooth and press, then sew the remaining binding strip.

5. Turn the folded edge of the binding to the back of the placemat and hand sew the edges down to conceal the raw edges. See figure 4 (front side) and figure 5 (reverse side).

Scrappy placemat is done! You have officially earned the right to go buy more fabric!

Figure 4

Figure 5

Appliqué placement (front)

Appliqué placement (back)

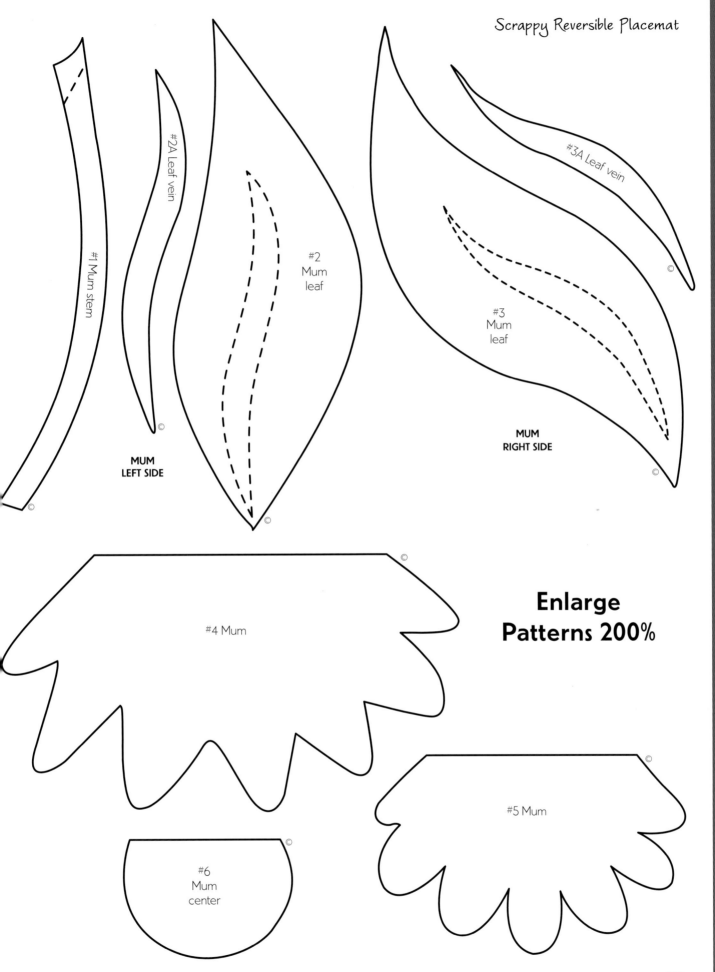

#2A Leaf vein

#3A Leaf vein

#1 Mum stem

#2
Mum
leaf

#3
Mum
leaf

MUM
LEFT SIDE

MUM
RIGHT SIDE

Enlarge
Patterns 200%

#4 Mum

#5 Mum

#6
Mum
center

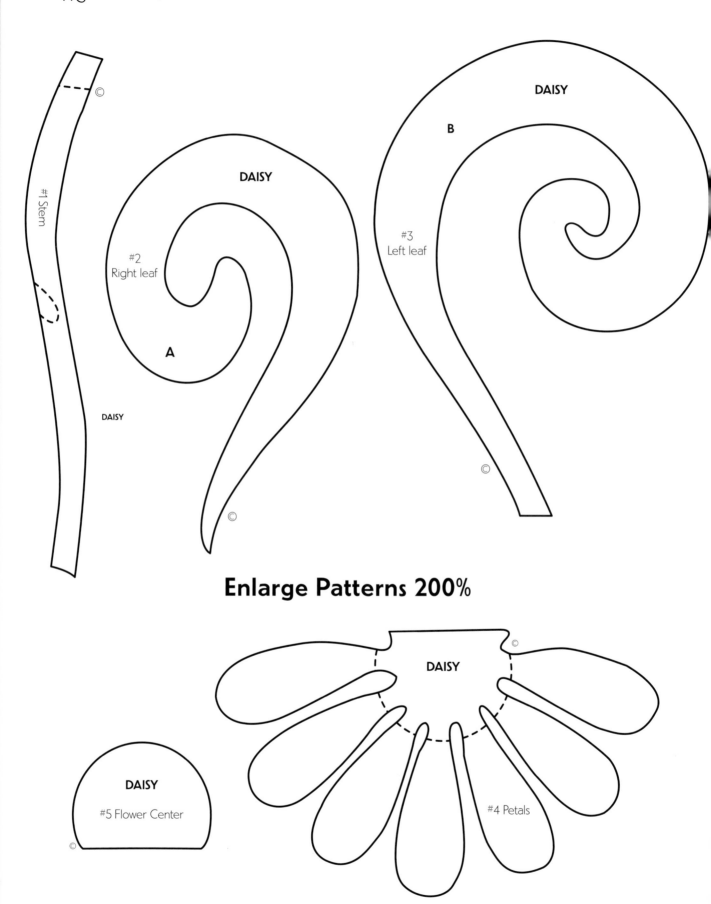

#1 Stem

DAISY

#2
Right leaf

A

DAISY

DAISY

B

#3
Left leaf

Enlarge Patterns 200%

DAISY

DAISY

#5 Flower Center

#4 Petals

SCRAPPY SHADES
Size varies

A little history on these babies: When I purchased my quilting machine, to my delight, you could order the sewing machine in colors!!! My dilemma—purple? red? or hot pink? Hmmmm. I went with pink.

My husband, upon discovering the substantial extra charge for color, took a huge gulp, and asked, "Honey, do you really need it to be painted another color?"

Scrappy Shade, made by author

Hello-o-o-o. The standard color was industrial gray. Let me tell you something: My laundry room walls are yellow-green with paintings of multicolored naked ladies in red frames hanging all around (they are waiting for their clothes to come out of the dryer). Gray????

So, the next issue was the light bar. It was black. The shades were black. Everything about it was black. I told them, no, thanks, my husband would make me a light fixture. Six months later, no light fixture, so I ordered the black light bar. Something had to be done with the black shades. They had to be fixed.

Note: These directions are for the small shades that came with my quilting machine, but with minor adjustments for different sizes, you can fix any shade.

Materials

Fabric scraps: about ¼ yard per shade (about .2 pound)

Foundation fabric: about 1 fat quarter

Beaded trim: about ¾ yard

Rickrack: about ⅓ yard

Other things:
- Lampshade in desperate need of a fix
- Removable ink fabric pen
- Spray adhesive
- Fabric glue (fast drying, dries clear; I like Fabri-Tac™.)

Directions

1. Find the seam on the lampshade. Place that seam on the foundation fabric.

2. Test by rolling the shade over the fabric starting with the seam and ending when you get to the seam again. You are making sure that you are able to stay within the boundaries of the fabric edges from the beginning to the end of the rolling process.

3. Again place the seam of the shade onto the foundation fabric. Mark the starting point where the seam meets both the top and bottom edges of the shade (figure 1). Slowly roll the shade across the fabric, marking the top and bottom edges as you go, ending when you get back to the seam (figure 2). Mark that point at the top and bottom, too.

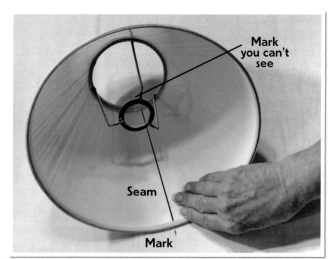

Mark you can't see

Seam

Mark

Figure 1

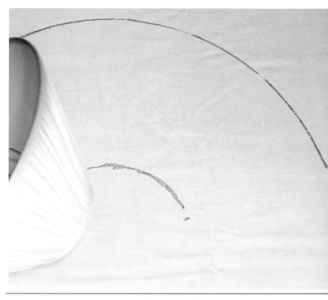

Figure 2

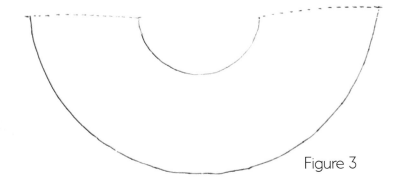

Figure 3

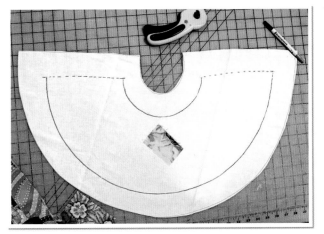

Figure 4

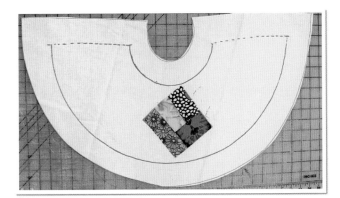

Figure 5

Figure 6

4. You should have a shape drawn on the fabric that looks a lot like a big fat letter C (figure 3). Now, add at least two inches all the way around the drawing on the fabric. Cut out this shape (figure 4).

5. Randomly select one small scrap (no larger than 2" x 3"). Place this scrap on top of the foundation fabric right-side up at an angle to the outer edge of the foundation shape (figure 4).

6. Place a second scrap right-side down on top of the first one with one set of edges aligned. Sew through all thicknesses. Open to expose the right sides of the scraps, press, and then trim any excess from the seam underneath (figure 5).

7. Rotate the foundation fabric one-quarter turn. Add another scrap to the first two, raw edges aligned. Stitch, press, trim.

8. Continue rotating the foundation fabric, adding additional scraps until all of the foundation fabric is covered (figure 6). Anytime you have a scrap that is too short, just sew another piece to it until it is long enough. No scrap is too small (well, almost) to use.

9. While it is not necessary, it is a good idea to do some kind of topstitching such as stippling or stitching in-the-ditch to keep the edges together.

Figure 7

Figure 8

Figure 9

10. From the reverse side, trim your pieced top back to the size of the foundation fabric (figure 7).

11. Go outside to spray the exterior of the lampshade with adhesive.

12. Once back inside, place the seam edge down on the back of the finished foundation/scrappy fabric piece. Roll the shade, smoothing and hand-pressing the fabric to the shade.

13. When you get all the way around, trim the end leaving about a 1" overlap.

14. Fold the end's raw edge to the inside and then use a small amount of fabric glue to seal the edge down.

15. Carefully trim the excess from the top and bottom of the shade (figure 8). Use a small amount of glue to secure any loose fabric along those edges.

16. Add the trim to the top and bottom edges starting at the seam side so all of the beginnings and endings are on the same side. Seal the ends of the trim with glue (figure 9).

Finally! The shade is dressed to impress.

TABLE SCRAPS

Actually, it is almost embarrassing to admit to the world just how many scraps I have. Oh, well, too late to go back now. So, this table runner was the result of my rummaging through my baskets, looking for other stuff. It has been a while since I stopped trying to separate my fabrics into batiks and non-batiks, darks and lights, vintage and designer, etc. It was hopeless to think that I could stay that organized. Anyway, it was fun revisiting my batiks and applying the same restrictions (no buying, use scraps) to this project. Now that I think about it, I probably should have taken a photograph of the scrap baskets "before the book" and then "after the book" to see if I could see a difference. (The photos in the book are "after" shots.)

Table Scraps, 21" x 49",
made by the author

Materials

<u>Main body:</u> The equivalent of 2 yards of as many different batik scraps as possible, half of lighter value, half of darker value (about ⅔ pound). Cut them into 5" half-square triangles (5" x 5" x 7¹⁄₁₆").

<u>Prairie points and binding:</u> ½ yard. I dipped into my stash in order to make this all the same fabric. It would be delightful to have different prints for the prairie points, so just have fun within your own parameters.

- Cut 1 strip 4" x the width of the fabric. Cut this strip into 8 squares 4" x 4".
- Cut 1 strip 4¼" x the width of the fabric. Cut 4 squares 4¼" x 4¼" from this strip.
- Cut the remaining 23" piece into 2 pieces 1¼" x 22½".
- From the remaining fabric cut 3 binding strips 2½" by the width of the fabric.

<u>Batting:</u> 23" x 51"

<u>Backing:</u> 1 yard

Main Body

1. Sew a lighter and a darker triangle together along the longer edges right-sides together. Open and press. Trim the square to 4" x 4" (figure 1). Repeat this step until you have 84 squares.

2. Stitch 2 of the 4" squares together along the edges of the darker triangles, right-sides facing in. Open and press. This makes a 4" x 7½" rectangle (figure 2). Continue sewing 2 squares together until all 84 of the 4" squares have been used. You should end up with 42 rectangles.

3. Sew 2 of these rectangles together along the darker edges to create a 7½" x 7½" block with a dark diamond in the center. Repeat until you have used all of the rectangles (figure 3). You should end up with 21 blocks.

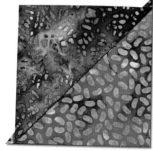

Figure 1

Figure 2

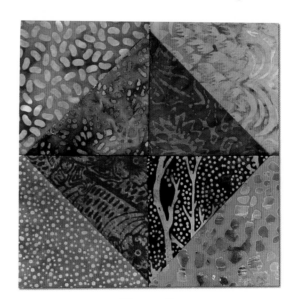

Figure 3

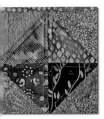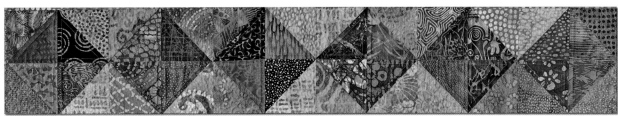

Figure 4

4. Sew 7 of these blocks together to get a row that is 7½" x 49½" (figure 4).

5. Make 2 more rows of 7 blocks. Sew the 3 rows together along the longer edges to make 1 piece 21½" x 49½".

6. Sandwich the top/batting/backing. Quilt. Trim the table runner to approximately 21" x 48" (figure 5).

Figure 5

Binding

1. Cut 1 of the 2½" x 40" binding strips in half (making 2 strips 2½" x 20"). Then sew 1 of these strips to each of the other two 2½" x 40" strips resulting in 2 strips 2½" x 60". Press the binding in half lengthwise.

2. Sew the binding to the quilt top along the two longer edges only. Trim to the length of the quilt (49½").

3. Turn the binding to the back of the quilt and hand stitch it in place.

Prairie Points

1. Press each of the 4" x 4" squares in half to form rectangles (figures 6 and 7). Do the same with the 4¼" x 4¼" squares.

2. Fold the outer edges up to form a point at the middle of the bottom, folded edge (figures 8 and 9). These are the prairie points. (It is very helpful to use Susan K. Cleveland's Prairie Pointer© to create these guys.)

3. These prairie points will be attached to the unfinished short edges of the quilt. The 4¼" prairie points should be placed on the outside edges (figures 10 [front] and 11 [back]). The 4" prairie points should be evenly spaced between these two (see the sample quilt photo on page 33). Baste them all in place.

4. Press ¼" under along the long edge of the 1¼" x 22½" binding piece. Pin it to the back side of the quilt with the right side of this strip facing the prairie points and raw edges aligned. Sew through all thicknesses.

5. Turn the excess to the inside, pressing and folding the binding and seam allowance to the back of the quilt. Hand stitch the binding in place.

6. Repeat these steps to finish the remaining edge.

Table Scraps is a feast for the eyes!

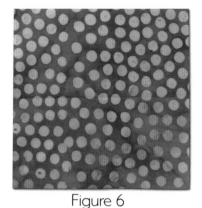

Figure 7

Figure 6

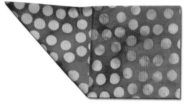

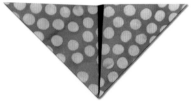

Figure 8

Figure 9

Figure 10

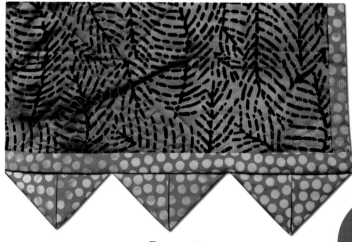

Figure 11

DAD'S DIAMONDS, 57" x 76½", made by the author

Dad's Diamonds

I got the idea for this quilt design from a pair of argyle socks that I began knitting for my dad many years ago. He was so excited that I was making them for him. He would have worn them on the outside of his shoes to show them off—if I had just finished them. So, my plan was to make this quilt so maybe I can get over my guilt for not finishing the socks. I think my dad would be proud.

This is by far the most challenging of the quilts in this book. It also has a bit of an extra cost because of the Quilt Smart® printed interfacing used as foundation piecing panels (you can find it at www.quiltsmart.com). Personally, I think it is worth not only the challenge but the cost. I love playing with Quilt Smart patterns. If you have not used this product before, I warn you, it is addictive.

Of course, you could make the 23 Lone Star diamonds according to your favorite method, so long as they measure 23" x 9½".

This quilt pattern definitely dipped into my stash in addition to my scrap pile. Still no noticeable difference in the scrap baskets—sigh.

Note: **Definitely read all the instructions before attempting this project.**

Materials

Foundation material: 12 Quilt Smart 38" Lone Star panel sets to make a total of 24 diamonds (they come in pairs). You only need 23, so you can use the leftover diamond on another project.

Scraps: 3¾ yards (about 1¼ pounds) of darker fabrics for 15 of the diamond shapes. 2 yards (⅔ pound) of light fabrics for the 8 other diamond shapes. The scraps need to be at least 2½" x 5½".

Stash: 1 yard to make the edge diamonds. There are 4 full diamonds at 23" x 9½", 8 triangles slightly larger than half-diamond size, and 4 corner triangles cut from half-diamonds.

Inner border: 2 strips 2½" x 63½" and 2 strips 2½" x 46½"

Outer border: 12 pieces of foundation fabric 12½" x 7½" and light scraps

Light fabrics: 1½ yards (½ pound) light value scraps for center and outer border

Binding: 1 strip 2½" x 280" made using dark scraps

Batting: Twin size (72" x 90")

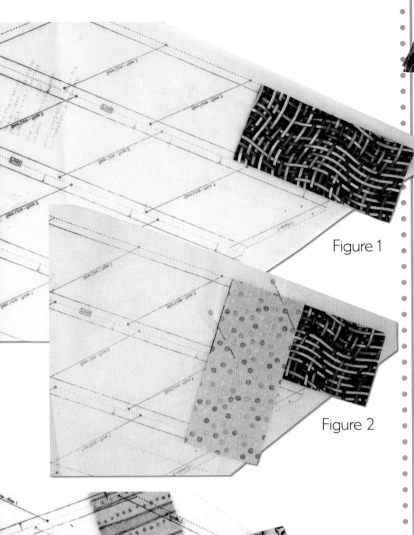

Figure 1

Figure 2

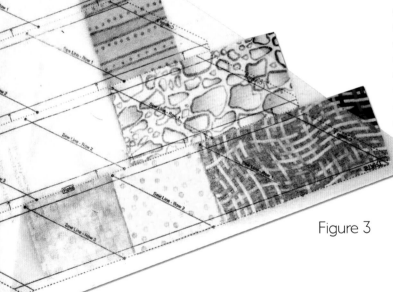

Figure 3

Center Diamonds

1. From the darker fabrics, cut 240 pieces each 2½" x 5½". Basically, we will be following the directions printed on the Quilt Smart. The difference is there will be no pattern to each diamond shape. The fabrics will be placed in a random order as far as color is concerned.

2. Look at each Quilt Smart diamond shape. The rough side is the side that receives the fabric. Place the first piece face up where the word "START" is printed. The longer edge of the fabric parallels the dotted line on the outer edge (figure 1).

3. Place a second piece on top of the first piece, right-sides together, perpendicular to the first one. Pin in place (figure 2).

4. Turn everything over and stitch where indicated on the Quilt Smart (figures 3 and 4).

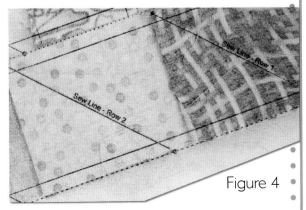

Figure 4

5. Turn the diamond back over so the fabric side is facing you. Press both fabrics in place. Add more fabric pieces (figure 5).

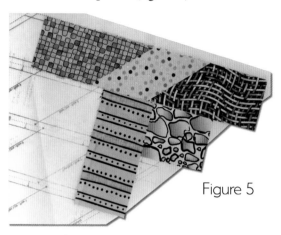

Figure 5

6. Continue adding fabrics in this manner until the whole piece of Quilt Smart is covered (figure 6).

7. Turn the diamond so the fabric side is face down. Fold and press on the dotted lines, then stitch on the solid lines. Open, press, and trim where indicated on the Quilt Smart. You have now cut a diamond (figure 7).

8. Repeat until you have 15 dark diamond shapes.

9. Next, repeat the previous steps for the remaining 8 diamond shapes using the light fabrics.

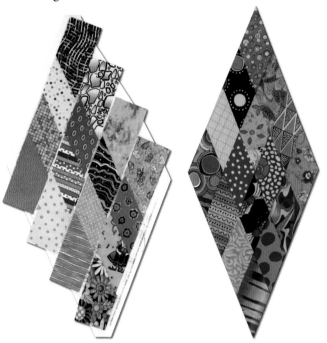

Figure 6   Figure 7

Outer Diamonds/Half Diamonds/ Quarter Diamonds

1. Use one of the completed, trimmed Quilt Smart diamond shapes as a template. Use a variety of light value background fabrics for this step. Cut 4 whole diamond shapes (figure 8).

2. The 8 half-diamond shapes are slightly larger than half of a whole diamond. Cut 1 whole diamond across slightly above the halfway point (figure 9). Then use this half diamond as a template to make 7 more.

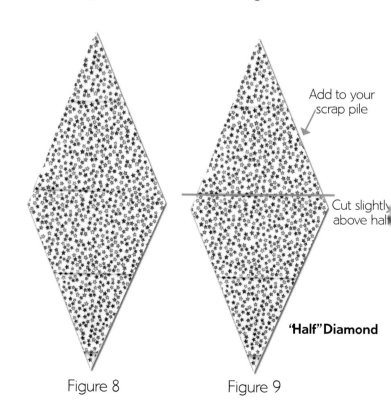

Add to your scrap pile

Cut slightly above half

"Half" Diamond

Figure 8   Figure 9

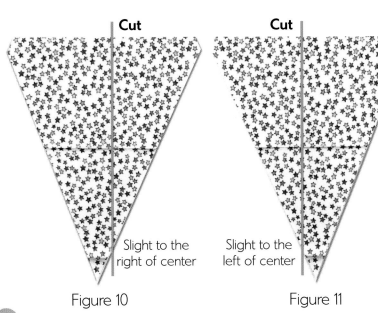

Cut

Slight to the right of center

Figure 10

Cut

Slight to the left of center

Figure 11

3. Cut 4 quarter-diamond shapes also slightly larger than one-fourth size. Using one of the half-diamond pieces above as a template, cut four more half diamonds. Then cut each of the four half diamonds into quarter diamonds (figures 10 and 11—make two of those each). The smaller piece left after the cut will be added to your scrap pile to help you with your next scrappy project. The larger of the two pieces will be the quarter diamond. This will give you one quarter diamond for each of the four corners.

Assembly

1. Sew the diamonds in diagonal rows (figure 12). Each diagonal row will begin and end with the outer diamonds/half diamonds/and quarter diamonds, as needed (figure 13).

2. Sew the rows together.

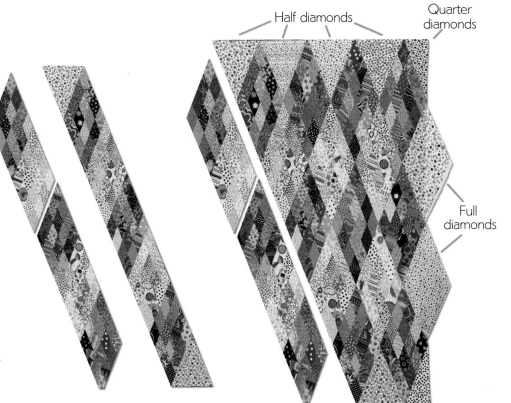

Half diamonds

Quarter diamonds

Full diamonds

Figure 12

Figure 13

Trimming

1. Square up the quilt using a long straight edge ruler.

2. Trim the outer edge to ¼" beyond the tips of all of the darker value diamond points (figure 14).

Inner Border

1. Add one of the 2½" x 63½" polka-dot strips to each of the longer edges of the quilt top.

2. Sew the remaining 2½" x 46½" strips to the top and bottom.

Outside Border Piecing

1. Place a square or rectangular scrap right-side up at an angle to the edges of 1 of the foundation pieces, in the approximate middle of the piece. This small rectangle or square should be no larger than, say, 3" x 3". The size is not terribly critical (figure 15).

2. Add a second scrap to the first by placing it right-sides together, longer edges aligned. Sew through all thicknesses. Flip so the right sides face up and press (figure 16).

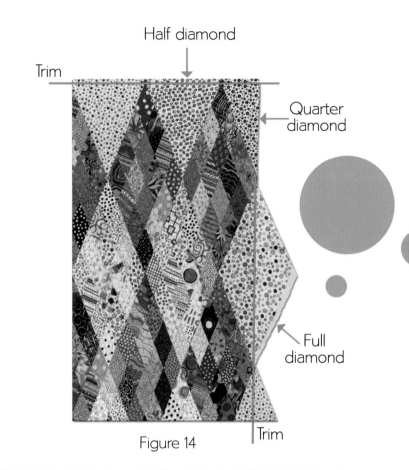

Figure 14

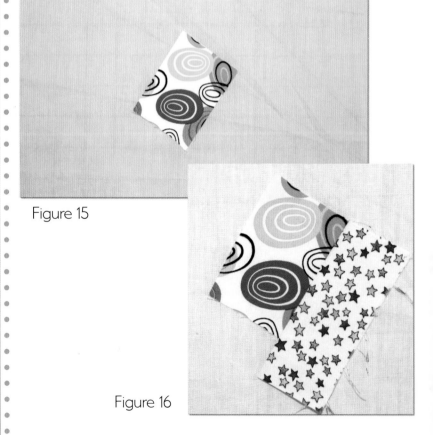

Figure 15

Figure 16

3. Turn the foundation piece 90 degrees and add a third strip. Sew. Trim excess fabric from underneath the scrappy strips so it will not get too bulky.

4. Continue adding pieces until the entire foundation piece is covered.

5. Complete all of the 22 foundation pieces in the same manner.

6. Trim 12 of the completed foundation pieces to 11½" x 6½" (figure 17). Sew 6 of these together to get a 66½" x 6½" strip. Repeat with the remaining 6. Set these 2 strips aside.

7. Trim 8 foundation pieces to 12½" x 6½". The last 2 need to be trimmed to 10½" x 6½".

8. Sew 2 strips 12½" x 6½" together along the 6½" sides. Add one of the 10½" x 6½" pieces, and then add two more 12½" pieces to this strip to make a 58½" long piece.

9. Repeat this for a second 58½" x 6½" piece.

Figure 17

Outer Border

1. Sew one of the 6½" x 66½" border strips to the sides of the quilt top.

2. Sew the 6½" x 58½" border strips to the top and bottom of the quilt top.

Binding

1. Cut 2½" dark scrap strips into a variety of lengths (12" – 18" long). Sew them together end to end until you have made a binding strip at least 280" long.

2. Sandwich the top/batting/backing. Quilt, trim, add binding, and smile!

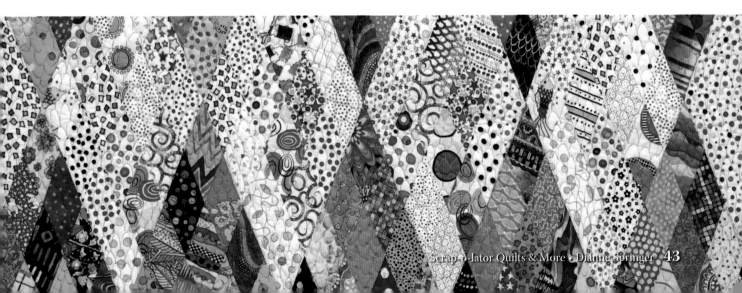

No-Sewing Projects

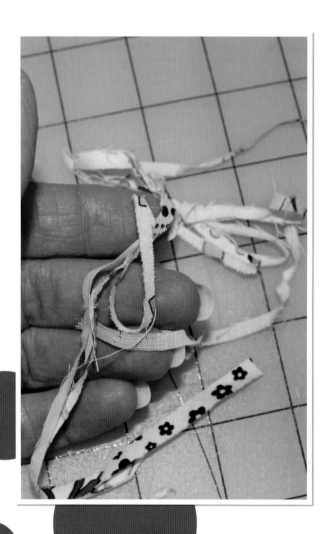

Fact #1: These projects are great for all ages, for those who sew and those who don't, the curious, the fun-seekers...

Fact #2: Nothing within my reach is safe from fabric.

Fact #3: You can never have too much Mod Podge®.

Fact #4: No piece of fabric is too small to keep. Well, I have been known to throw out pieces like those in the photo. Then my daughter discovered she could weave them into—um, wait—that just might be the next book...

QUILT ON A RUG

Quilt on a Rug, 7' x 6', made by the author

Please note that your rug does not have to be a rectangle. It could be a heart shape, a circle, irregular, etc. Be creative! However, these directions are based on a 7' x 6' rectangular shape plus 1" on each side for hemming later. Most folks will not want a rug that large, so my directions are, I hope, adjustable to suit your needs.

Note: As happy as I am to talk about almost anything, please read all of the directions for this project before beginning it and calling me with questions. If you do have questions, call me at 318-247-9725.

Quilt on a Rug

Materials

Artist's canvas—preferably pre-primed*:
3 yards of 60" wide canvas or cotton duck or Multi-Purpose Cloth™**

Mod Podge: (I prefer a satin finish so the rug still appears "quilty")

Fabric scraps, varied sizes and shapes: LOTS

Outer border fabric: 2½ yards for a 7' rug

Inner border fabric: 2 yards

Other things:
- Steam-A-Seam 2
- Superfine sandpaper, about 300 grit (sanding sponges work well)

- Water-based varnish (satin finish Minwax® water-based polyurethane or polycrylic works well)
- Scallop template (optional)
- Paint brush
- Scissors
- Pencil
- Ruler
- Iron
- Tape
- Several sheets of typing paper or a large sheet of newsprint or butcher paper
- 1 cheap white muslin sheet and Stitch Witchery® (optional)
- Teflon® or silicone pressing sheet

* Add gesso to your supply list if the canvas is not pre-primed
**(MPC is pre-primed on both sides)

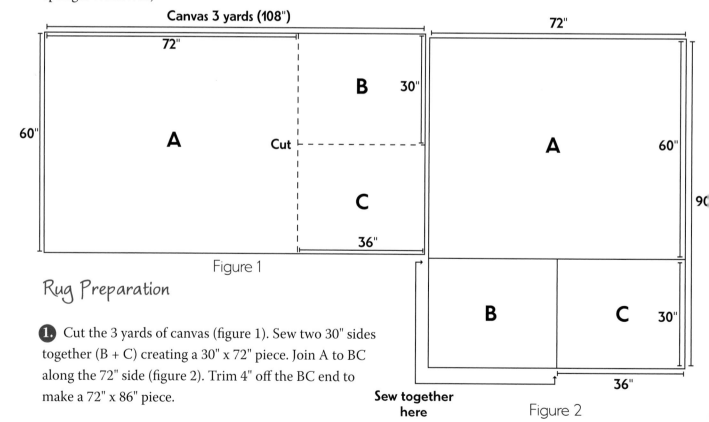

Figure 1

Figure 2

Sew together here

Rug Preparation

1. Cut the 3 yards of canvas (figure 1). Sew two 30" sides together (B + C) creating a 30" x 72" piece. Join A to BC along the 72" side (figure 2). Trim 4" off the BC end to make a 72" x 86" piece.

2. If the canvas is not already primed, paint one side with gesso following the manufacturer's directions. When dry, sand lightly. Be sure to wipe off the dust from sanding with a damp cloth.

Border Preparation

1. Please note that my border is not perfect. It is made up of several pieces of fabric; I adjusted it as I went. If you want a border as seen in the picture, you may either follow the directions that come with the scallop template, or follow the directions below (I was a school teacher, so I usually had to figure a way to avoid buying stuff like the template. My method might be a bit more trouble, but it allows for more creativity.)

2. Tape several sheets of typing paper end-to-end to cover a section of the rug (figure 3). Be sure to tape these on both sides as you will be flipping them around.

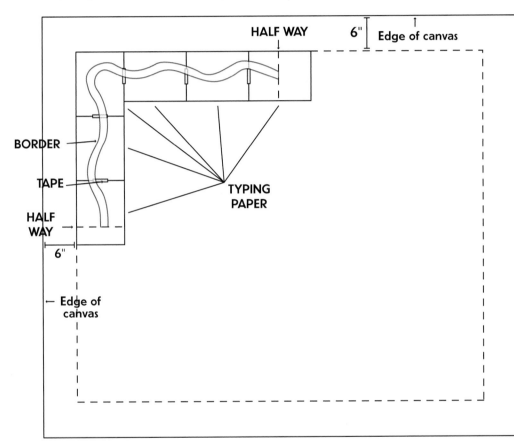

Figure 3

3. Now tape this group of papers to the canvas, lining it up with the outside edges 6" in from the edges of the canvas.

4. Mark the half-way point of the rug on the typing paper and the canvas.

5. Repeat this on the width edge. Find and mark the half-way points of the remaining two edges.

6. Trim a piece of cardboard 4" x the width you want your border (mine is 3" wide so that would make it a 4" x 3" piece) and tape 2 pencils to the outside edges (figure 4). If your cardboard is flimsy, tape at least two pieces together before adding the pencils. This contraption is something that helps keep the border consistent in width and it allows you to draw both sides of the border at the same time.

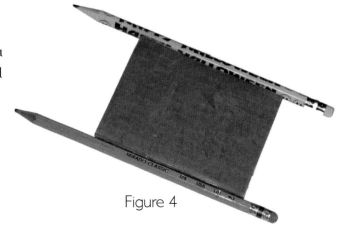

Figure 4

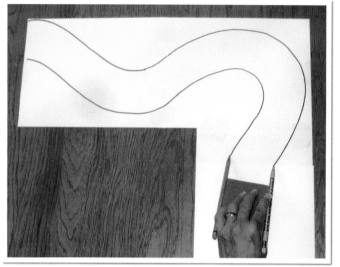

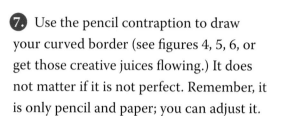

Figure 5

7. Use the pencil contraption to draw your curved border (see figures 4, 5, 6, or get those creative juices flowing.) It does not matter if it is not perfect. Remember, it is only pencil and paper; you can adjust it.

8. When you are happy with this shape, cut it out, tape it back down on the canvas matching the half-way points, and draw around it with a pencil.

9. Flip the pattern over and trace around it, again. Repeat this flip-and-draw method until you are all the way around the rug (figure 6).

10. This paper pattern is also the pattern for cutting out your fabric for the border. If your border is a light colored fabric, as mine was (yellow with red dots), back the fabric before cutting it out to make it more opaque. The cheapest way to do this is to buy the least expensive white muslin sheet you can find. Bond it to the back of your border fabric using Steam-A-Seam 2 or Stitch Witchery.

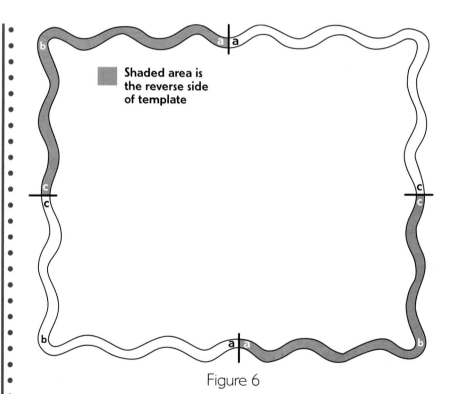

Shaded area is the reverse side of template

Figure 6

11. Now, use your pattern to cut out your border fabric(s). You will need to draw the pattern twice from the front and twice from the reversed side (back) so you will have enough to go all the way around AND have it going in the right direction. Remember, we only drew off ¼ of the length around. Truthfully, you can cut your border in as many pieces as you need. No one will notice if it looks right.

Make the Rug

1. Starting in the center of the canvas, paint glue (Mod Podge) over an area slightly larger than the first piece of fabric. Place the fabric down on the glue and paint more glue on top, covering the entire piece of fabric.

2. Paint more glue in an area adjacent to the first piece of fabric. Place the second fabric on that glue, slightly overlapping one edge of the first fabric. Again, cover this fabric with glue.

3. Continue gluing and adding pieces of fabric in the same manner until the entire center of the rug is covered.

4. If you do not have a border, the fabric should go all the way to the edge of the canvas. If you do have a border, take the center fabrics just over the inner edge of the border (the line you drew with the pencil).

5. Now, starting with the outside edge of the canvas, apply pieces of fabric until you have covered just over the outer edge of the drawn border. You should have a small area that is not covered with fabric that goes all the way around the rug. That is your border area.

6. Glue the border pieces down using the same technique you used for applying the rest of the fabrics. You may need to trim or adjust the border pieces to completely cover the exposed area.

7. Let the rug dry overnight.

8. Paint a coat of varnish over the entire rug. When that is dry, sand the surface lightly with the superfine sandpaper. Remove all of the dust with a damp cloth.

9. Paint at least 2 more coats of varnish over the entire rug, alternating brush stroke direction for each coat. Follow manufacturer's directions for use and clean up.

10. When it is completely dry, turn the rug so that the back faces up. Place the Teflon pressing sheet between the rug and the ironing board. Iron the strips of Steam-A-Seam 2 to the outermost edge of the rug, moving the protective sheet as you work around the entire edge. Remove the adhesive paper.

11. Fold approximately 1" of the rug to the back and wrap the edge with the Teflon sheet to protect both sides of the rug. Hold the iron in place for 8-10 seconds, then lift it and press the adjacent area (do NOT slide the iron.)

12. Do not remove the protective sheet until the rug has cooled completely. Patience is a virtue. If you are making a curved edge rug, such as a heart shape or oval, you will need to clip the curved edges of the hem to make it lie flat.

QUILT ON A LAMP

Quilt on a Lamp,
total height 29",
made by the author

Crazy as it may sound, I get these ideas, and when I recall them, it is like I have a map in my brain for where the ideas are located. For this one, drive north...

Note: The measurements on this project will vary depending on the size and shape of your lamp and lampshade. Please measure carefully and adjust.

Materials

Fabric scraps for the base: approximately ½ yard total (about .4 pound) including strips of a black-and-white stripe, or check, or polka dot for the accents (mainly, the concern is for using a strong contrasting accent fabric)

Fabric for lampshade: 1⅓ yards (a generous ⅓ pound)

Trim for the edges: 1⅓ yards for the bottom edge plus ⅜ yard for top edge (½ pound) (You could use 2 different kinds of trim, which increases the possibility of using scraps or sale items)

Fabric for flowers: 8" squares of 6 fabrics

Leaf fabrics: 1 square 10" x 10" of at least 2 different greens for the leaves

Directions

1. Lightly sand the body of the lamp base. Use a damp cloth to wipe off the dust. With a sponge brush, apply *slightly* diluted Mod Podge to the lamp over an area a little larger than the first fabric scrap you are using. Be sure to pay attention to any decorative parts to make sure glue is everywhere, particularly in the creases.

2. Add a piece of fabric, pushing it into the indentions/decorative areas. Re-apply glue to the top of the fabric and the surrounding areas. Add more fabric, overlapping the edges of the first piece where possible (figure 1).

3. Continue adding glue and fabric until the entire base is covered. Wait until this layer is dry before adding the decorative trim. It is easy to miss spots

Stitch Witchery or Wonder-Under®: 1 yard

Other things:
- Lamp base (this one I purchased for $5 from a second-hand store, a.k.a., junk shop)
- Mod Podge
- Brushes: both sponge and bristle
- Varnish: gloss if you want it to look like ceramic, matt if you want to retain the look of fabric
- Sandpaper
- Beaded stamens (from the bridal department)
- Florist wire or heavy-duty thread
- Lampshade with adhesive (available from craft stores, or, you can use a spray adhesive on a regular lampshade)
- Marking pen/pencil with removable/disappearing ink
- Clear-drying glue (I prefer Fabri-Tac because it dries quickly and it dries clear)

Figure 1

and, for some unexplained reason, it seems easier to catch them when the piece is dry. So, don't worry about it; just add more fabric to the empty spots before adding the trim.

Trim

1. Measure around the area where you want the contrasting fabric and add 1". My lamp measured 21" at the widest part, so I cut a piece 22" x ½". I also used a piece of the contrasting fabric around the upper part of the lamp. Measure around that area and add about 1" to that measurement x ½". The very top of the lamp uses the measurement around plus about ½" x the height of that area (mine was 3" x 2¼"). If you are using a stripe, try to end the overlap so it completes a stripe as much as possible. This disguises the "end" as much as you can (figure 2).

2. After everything is completely dry, lightly sand the entire piece. Use a damp cloth to wipe off the dust.

3. Carefully stir the varnish, trying not to create bubbles. Use the bristle or sponge brush to apply the varnish. I usually start at the top and work my way to the bottom. Again, do not worry if you did not get every single inch covered. It is better to do several light coats rather than apply too much at one time and get drips. Luckily drips can be sanded and lightly re-varnished. Wait until this dries completely.

4. Lightly sand, wipe, and recoat with the varnish. Repeat until you have at least three coats. The more coats, the smoother the finish.

Figure 2

> **Hint:** It is not necessary to clean the brush each time, or to use a new one if you are using the disposable kind. Just take a plastic bag, even the cheapie shopping bags will do, put the brush inside, preferably with the handle outside, and squish all the air out from around the bristles. Put that whole thing inside another cheapie bag. Squish out the air. This keeps the brush moist until you are done with the piece.

Lampshade

If you are using a shade without the sticky coating, follow these directions; otherwise, skip to Step 4*.

1. On the inside of the shade, look for the seam (figure 3). You will be using this seam as the starting and stopping points. Test for the best place to start rolling the shade over the fabric so you will begin and end without going over the edge of the fabric. Now, using a removable pen, mark on the wrong side of the fabric where the seam on the shade begins (figure 4).

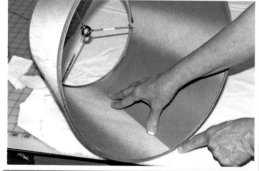

Figure 3

Figure 4

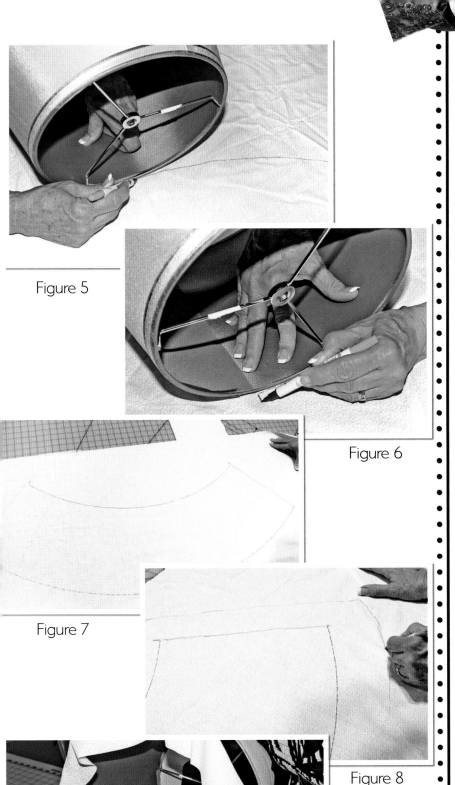

Figure 5

Figure 6

Figure 7

Figure 8

Figure 9

2. Be sure to mark both the top and bottom edges. Roll the shade over the fabric, marking the top and bottom edges as you go (figure 5). When you get back around to the seam, mark that point (figure 6).

3. You should have a shape marked on the fabric that looks like a big fat letter C (figure 7). Add at least 2" on all sides, all the way around this shape (figure 8). Cut out this shape.

4. Go outside to spray the adhesive all over the wrong side of the fabric. Go back inside and lay the fabric glue-side up.

4*. If you are using a shade with a sticky coating, use the protective sheet that comes on the shade as a template for the shade. You will still need to add at least 2" all the way around the drawn shape. Cut out on the outer shape line. Place the fabric wrong side up on the table.

5. Carefully, lay the shade down on the fabric, matching the markings for the seam. Now, roll, smoothing and pressing the fabric with your hand. When you are all the way around, trim, leaving a small over-lap. It might help to have someone assist you. Apply a small bit of glue to the raw edge and smooth that out.

6. Now, trim the top and bottom edges of the fabric even with the shade (figure 9).

Quilt on a Lamp

7. Place a line of glue partway around the upper edge of the shade on the outside. Add your decorative trim and hold it in place with clamps (figure 10).

8. Add more glue and trim until you have gone all the way around. Repeat for the bottom edge. I usually start and stop the trim at the same place that the fabric started and stopped so that is all at the "back" of the shade. This trim often has multiple decorative threads, cords, etc., so be sure to add a small amount of glue to those ends to make them stay down and lessen their visibility. Another approach is to start and stop your trim where

Figure 10

any flowers will go so that all ends are hidden behind the flowers and/or leaves.

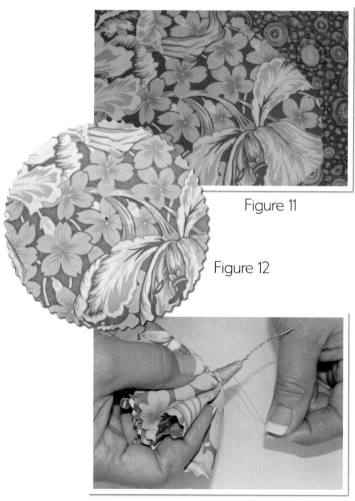

Figure 11

Figure 12

Figure 13

Flowers

1. Use two of the 8" squares and 1 piece of the bonding material to heat set the two fabrics together, right-sides out (figure 11). Use one of the flower circle templates on page 55 as a pattern and pinking shears or a rotary cutter with a pinking blade to cut out a circle from the bonded fabric. Fold the circle in half and then into a quarter circle to find the middle (figure 12).

2. Poke a tiny hole in the center and push the wires of the beaded stamen into the hole. Pinch and gather the flower material up from the bottom to form a flower. Wrap the base of the flower with either florist wire or heavy-duty thread (figure 13). Tie off and then trim the excess stamen wires. Repeat this series of steps until you have two smaller flowers and one larger flower.

Leaves

1. For the leaves, bond the two 10" squares together in the same manner as the flower fabrics. Trace at least 2 of each of the leaf shapes below and cut them out on the line (total of at least 6 leaves). Overlap and glue the tip of each leaf (figure 14).

2. Trim one of the sides that extends even with the outer edge of the leaf. These leaves are reversible and are intended to be used with either side as the right side.

3. Glue the flowers in place first and then add the leaves. Use the leaves to help hide the base of the flowers. Add additional beaded stamens (figure 15).

Now, this project did not make even a tiny dent in your stash pile but it was a delight to do, don't you think?

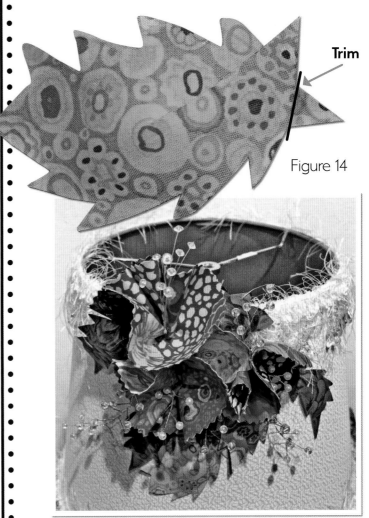

Trim

Figure 14

Figure 15

Enlarge Patterns 200%

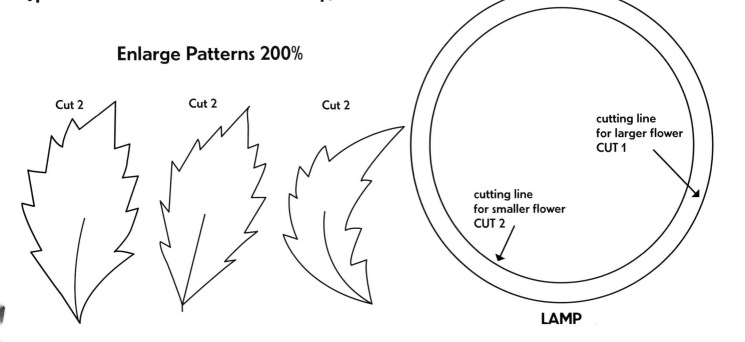

Cut 2

Cut 2

Cut 2

cutting line for larger flower CUT 1

cutting line for smaller flower CUT 2

LAMP

QUILT ON A CHAIR

Totally fun project. I love to transform an ordinary object into something that attracts attention, and these babies do exactly that.

OK—a little sewing is involved, but you can handle it.

Quilt on a Chair,
made by the author

Materials

<u>Foundation fabric:</u> 1 yard (⅓ pound) of an inexpensive sheet or any other medium-weight white fabric

<u>Fun fabrics:</u> Approximately 1 yard of scraps (⅓ pound) for both the seat and back of the chair. It is a good idea for these to be trimmed so they have straight edges. I trim my scraps stacked several at a time, varying the length and width with each group. You will also need ¼ yard of striped fabric (.2 ounces) cut into 3 strips 2" wide x the width of the fabric. Sew these together for 1 long strip to be used on both top and bottom.

<u>Traditional sewing supplies</u>

<u>Chair:</u>   I bought these folding metal chairs at the local discount store. I loved the possibilities of the flat black color but I think it would be great to paint them a wild color, as well.

<u>Fast-drying glue:</u>   (I love Fabri-Tac) or a hot-glue gun and glue sticks

<u>Staple gun and staples:</u> (Be sure to test the staples to avoid having them be too long and poke through the seat into the fanny—ouch)

Making the Covers

1. Remove the screws that hold the cushions onto the seat and back of the chair. If the chair has brads instead of screws, simply drill out the brads and replace them with screws when reattaching the cushions. You do not need to remove the existing fabric covers unless they are a thick, heavy material.

2. Measure the width and length of the cushions. Add at least 3" to the measurement on all 4 sides to allow for wrapping fabric over the edge of the cushion (figure 1). Also, it is wise to have this new cover extend longer than the original (if you chose to leave the original cover on) so all the bulk from the two covers is not ending at the same place. It is easier to trim off the excess than to have it come up short. Voice of experience…

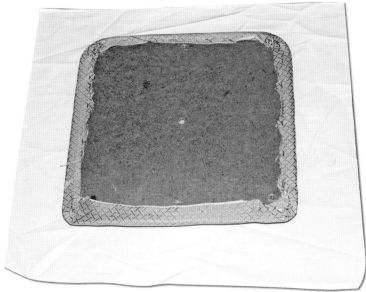

Figure 1

3. Cut a piece of the foundation fabric to the measurement of the seat cushion (with the extra 3" on all sides, of course.) My chair bottom measured 16" x 16" so I cut my fabric 22" x 22".

Quilt on a Chair

4. Place one of your fabric scraps cut to approximately 2" x 3" (as is the case with many of my projects, these are NOT critical measurements) on the foundation fabric, in the middle, right-side up, at an angle to the outermost edges (figure 2).

5. Sew a second piece to one of the longer sides of this 3" piece, right-sides together, through all thicknesses. Open, press, and trim excess from under the seam or where the second piece extends past the first piece of fabric (figure 3).

6. Turn 90 degrees clockwise or counterclockwise and sew a third piece right-side down, through all thicknesses (figure 4). Open, press, and trim.

7. Turn 90 degrees and add another piece in the same manner. Continue adding fabric strips until the entire foundation piece is completely covered.

8. Now is the time to add decorative stitches or couch over some ribbon, or yarn, or cording, etc. Trim to the original size of the foundation fabric.

9. Repeat these steps for the back cushion.

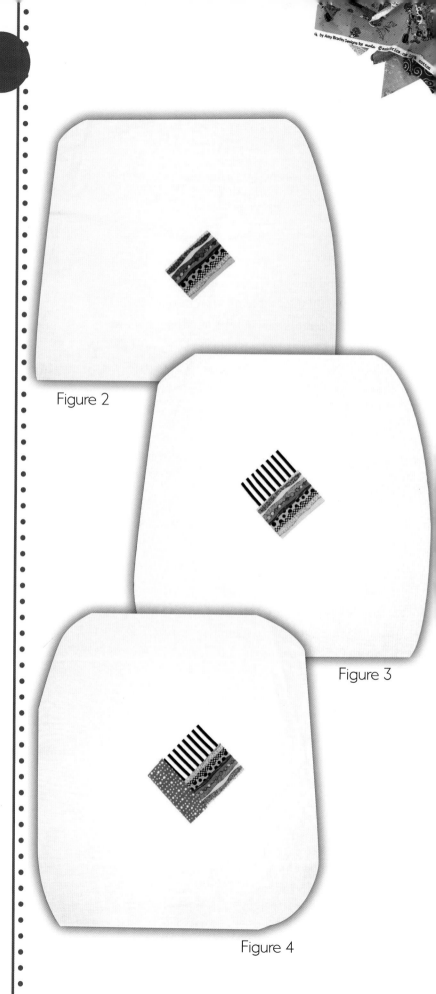

Figure 2

Figure 3

Figure 4

Covering the Cushions

Note: Work by adding only a few staples at a time. In other words, do not start on one side and staple all of that side and move around the entire bottom in that manner. You should put one or two staples in one side, and then move to the opposite side of the cushion to add more staples.

Figure 5

Figure 6

1. Center the pieced foundation (we'll call it a quilt even though it isn't one) on the chair cushion. Carefully invert the quilt and cushion so the bottom of the cushion is facing up. Fold one of the outer edges of the quilt up and over the edge of the cushion. Put one or two staples in the center of one edge of the quilt square. Carefully stretch the quilt and put one or two staples in the opposite edge of the quilt square/ cushion (figure 5).

2. Move to one of the remaining edges and place one or two staples in that edge. Now, stretch the quilt and staple the last edge with one or two staples placed in the center of that edge.

3. Continue adding only a few staples at a time to each edge, until you get a few inches from the corners. At this point it is a good idea to stretch the fabric over the outermost edge of a corner and staple that first. You may need to trim some of the bulk.

4. Go to the opposite corners and staple. Continue as before, adding a few staples at a time, smoothing gathers at the corners (figure 6).

5. Repeat this method with the chair back.

6. Take one end of the striped strip and press it under ½". If you have not already done so, press the strip in half lengthwise, right-sides out. Starting about 2" from the end that you pressed under, stitch the raw edges together in a ¼" seam along the entire length.

7. With the folded edge of the striped piece to the outside, test to see how much of the strip that you want to show from under the cushion (figure 7). This is a trial and error method. You will need to rest the seat cushion on top because it will probably push the trim down more than you realize. Remove the cushion and set it aside.

8. Start gluing the striped piece to the metal chair using either the Fabri-Tac or the glue gun. I like to use the Fabri-Tac simply because you have a little more time to adjust as you go. If you prefer, you may glue this trim directly to the bottom of the seat cushion. I had better luck gluing it directly to the metal. Again, this is just a personal preference.

9. When you get all the way around the seat, cut the striped piece about 1" too long. Tuck this end between the folded edge of where you started, hiding the raw edge inside the edge you pressed under ½" (figure 7). Finish gluing.

10. Re-attach the seat cushion with the original screws.

11. Follow steps 7-11 for the chair back. You will need to remove about two inches of stitching from one end of the striped trim. Press under ½" at this end. This will, again, be your starting edge when applying the trim.

Makes you want to do another one, doesn't it? That's why I have several!!!

Hint: Start gluing the striped piece from the edge that was pressed under ½". Also, I like to make this starting/stopping place as unnoticeable as possible, so I placed this at the side edge near the back.

Tuck inside to hide raw edge

Fold

¼ inch seam

Figure 7

MANIC MAILBOX

Manic Mailbox, 20¾" x 25¾",
made by the author

This is definitely a "far out" project—far out of your house, at least.
If creating envy amongst your neighbors makes you sleep well at
night, get some new sheets, some new jammies, and a great pillow
because you are gonna be in Nighty Night Heaven.

Note: While the mailbox I used was a "standard" oversized one,
there is a good possibility that the mailbox you use will not be the
same size as the one used for these directions. Please adjust your
measurements accordingly.

Manic Mailbox

Materials

Fabric: ½ yard of 54" fabric
Approximately ½ yard of fabric scraps (about .4 pound)

Other things:
- Mailbox
- Multi-Purpose Cloth (MPC) (size depends on the measurements of your mailbox)
- Mod Podge

- Sponge brush
- Bristle brush
- Roll of magnetic strips
- Acrylic
- Sanding block
- Glue such as Fabri-Tac
- Tape measure, scissors/rotary cutter, pencil, small bowl

Optional: 1 can of spray paint, color of your choice

Directions

1. If the color of the mailbox is not satisfactory, remove the hardware and flag, sand the box lightly, remove the dust with a damp cloth, and then spray paint the mailbox paying particular attention to the back of the box, the door, and its surrounding area. It is a nice touch to paint the inside of the door as well.

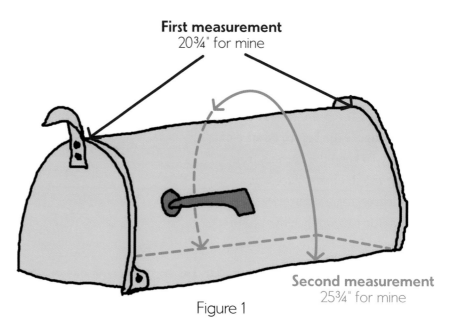

First measurement
20¾" for mine

Second measurement
25¾" for mine

Figure 1

2. With the door closed measure from the edge of the door to the inside edge of the back (figure 1). The measurement for my box was 20¾". Take the measurement from the bottom edge of one side of the box up and over the top to the bottom edge of the other side of the box. (For my box, the measurement was 25¾").

3. Cut a piece of MPC at least 2" larger than the length and width (for my box that meant 22¾" x 27¾").

4. With the sponge brush, apply Mod Podge (that has been very slightly thinned with water) to an area on the MPC slightly larger than the first piece of fabric. Place the fabric on top of the adhesive and then apply more Mod Podge on top of the fabric. Thinning the Mod Podge allows the glue to soak into the fabric a little more easily.

5. Apply more glue, then add another piece of fabric overlapping edges of the first piece of fabric. Paint over the second fabric with more glue.

6. Add a third fabric in the same manner (figure 2). Continue adding fabric until the entire MPC is covered. Let dry.

Figure 2

7. Sand lightly with the sanding block. Wipe off any dust with a damp cloth. Carefully stir the varnish. Using a bristle brush, cover the entire MPC. Let dry.

8. Sand lightly and remove the dust. Add two more layers of varnish, sanding between layers.

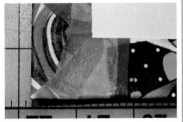

Figure 3

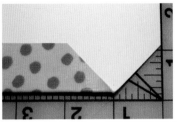

Figure 4

9. Mark 1" from all of the outside edges and fold to the inside, essentially "hemming" the outside edges (figure 3). Test to be sure of the fit. To keep the corners from being too thick, cut excess at a 45-degree angle (figure 4). Use Fabri-Tac to glue the edges to the inside.

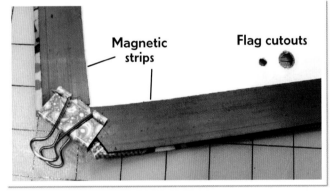

Magnetic strips

Flag cutouts

Figure 5

10. Peel the protective tape from the magnetic strip. Apply it to all hemmed edges. Put your Manic Mailbox cover onto the mailbox. You might have to add some glue to the self-adhesive magnetic strip and clamp it until the glue dries (figure 5).

Figure 6

Cut cover here for flag and hinges

11. Cut out areas for hinges and the hole for the flag (figures 6 and 7). Reattach the hardware and flag.

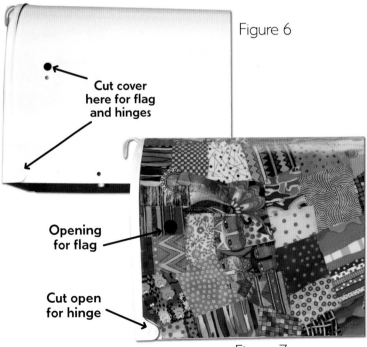

Opening for flag

Cut open for hinge

I feel neighborly envy building even as we speak...

Figure 7

PRETTY PIGGY

This not just a pretty pig, it is a bank. (I do love "form and function"). You have now saved so much $$ by using up your scraps for all of these fun projects that you just might need to make two of these babies. I cannot even remember where I first saw a paper-mache version of this bank because I made my first one more than 40 years ago for my daughter, Brandy. I only recently decided to dress the bank up with fabrics. Don't be intimidated by the long list of ingredients—just have fun!!

Pretty Piggy, 10" x 13", made by the author

Note: Read the directions all the way through before starting. This is a great weekend project. However, once started, you should finish the paper-layering phase within 24 hours, otherwise, the balloon will start to shrivel.

Materials

<u>Scraps:</u>   amount depends on the size of your pig

<u>Ribbon:</u> 1½ yards of ¼" ribbon for the tail

<u>Other things:</u>
- Balloon (at least 12" in diameter)
- Paper-mache or wallpaper paste such as Bondex®, or a flour/water mixture of 2 parts flour to 1 part water
- Newspaper, newsprint, and/or paper towels torn (NOT cut) into pieces, around 1"–2" across

- Bowl of water
- Small bowls
- Cardboard egg carton
- Masking tape
- Fabric
- Mod Podge
- Stopper (cork or rubber)
- Sponge brush and a super cheap bristle brush
- Sanding block
- Rags, pencil, Exacto® knife, scissors
- MinWax (water-based polycrylic; I prefer a satin finish)
- Fabri-Tac
- Buttons for eyes

Make the Pig

1. Prepare glue by thoroughly mixing the flour and water together in one of the bowls or follow directions on the wallpaper paste box. Mixture should be the consistency of heavy cream.

2. Tear the newsprint or paper towel into small pieces. Believe it or not, smaller is better, and quicker, than larger pieces. Blow up the balloon to desired size. (You might find it helpful to set the balloon in a small bowl to hold it steady while applying layers.)

3. Dip a piece of the newsprint into the bowl of water (not glue) and place it on the balloon (figure 1). The water makes it cling to the balloon. Add additional pieces of paper making sure you overlap the edges of the previous paper pieces. Continue adding paper until the entire balloon is covered (figure 2). This layer keeps the balloon from sticking to the paper-mache once the project is finished.

Figure 1

Figure 2

Pretty Piggy

4. The next layer of paper uses the glue. Dip a piece of newspaper into the bowl of glue and wipe off the excess. You want the paper wet, not dripping or globbed with glue. If you use an excessive amount of glue, it will mold before drying, and, your balloon will shrivel, so be careful to squeegee each piece of paper between your fingers to remove the excess glue. Place these pieces on the first layer of paper (figure 3).

5. Completely cover the balloon with the gluey paper making sure you overlap the edges of previous pieces (figure 4).

6. For the second glued layer, use a contrasting paper such as paper towels, blank newsprint, or the color comic pages from the Sunday paper. This makes it easier to see where you have covered. Be sure to keep a record of the layers because it is very easy to get confused as to how many layers you have completed.

7. Alternate blank/printed paper glue layers until there are *at least* 5 layers of glued paper (remember, don't count the first, water-only layer). Let dry for several hours. It helps to use a fan to speed the drying process. While this is drying, prepare the ears, nose, and feet.

8. Separate 7 cups from the egg carton. Four of these will be the feet, one will be the nose, and two will be the ears (figure 5).

9. To make the ears, take two of the cups and mark them as shown in (figure 6). Then cut along the marking. Keep the part indicated. Precision is not in order here. Ever seen a pig's ear?

Figure 3

Figure 4

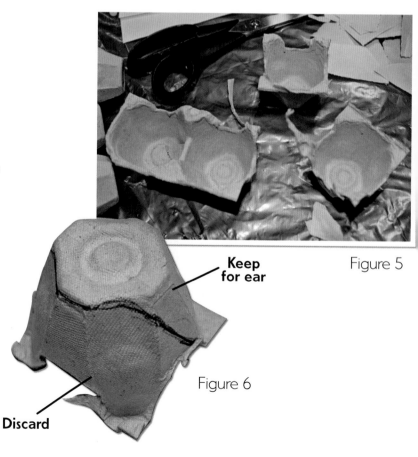

Keep for ear

Figure 5

Discard

Figure 6

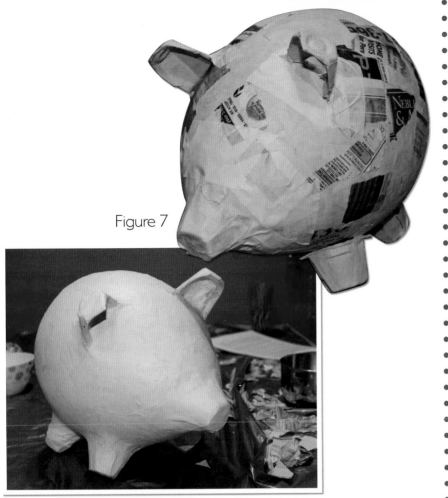

Figure 7

Figure 8

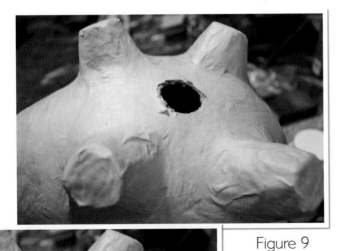

Figure 9

Figure 10

10. As soon as the glue is dry on the balloon, attach the feet, ears, and nose with masking tape (figure 7). Put the "nose" on the knot end of the balloon and make sure there is room between the feet for the stopper. Adjust the feet as needed to make Pretty Piggy stand evenly.

11. Apply at least five more layers of paper/glue to the entire piggy, including the feet, ears, and nose. You might want to add a few extra layers around the feet where they attach to the body. Allow each layer to dry for at least 30 minutes to prevent the previous layers from becoming overly wet. The last layer should be a light, preferably unprinted paper (figure 8). Let dry completely.

12. Turn Pretty Piggy over and trace the outline of the small end of the stopper on bottom of her tummy between the feet. Use the Exacto knife to carefully cut out the hole for the stopper. Be sure to cut the hole smaller than the outline you drew. You can always make the hole larger, but not smaller (figure 9).

13. Test the fit of the stopper and adjust as needed (figure 10). When you are satisfied with the fit, use tiny pieces of paper and some Mod Podge glue to finish the edges of the stopper hole.

Figure 11

14. Use an Exacto knife to cut a deposit slit in the top (figure 11). The slot should be approximately 1 ½" x ¼"). Finish the edges as done earlier for the stopper.

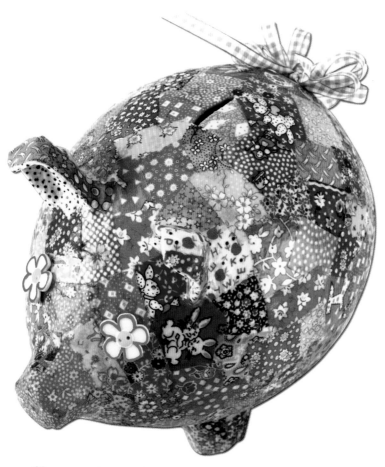

Use Your Scraps

1. Using the Mod Podge and a small sponge brush, apply glue to a portion of the body. Place a piece of fabric on top of the glued area. Paint over the fabric with more glue. Add more fabric, with edges overlapping the first fabric. Then apply more glue over that. Continue until you have covered the entire bank with small pieces of fabric, overlapping edges as you go.

2. When completely dry, lightly sand the surface. Wipe off dust with a damp rag.

3. Remove lid from the MinWax and stir it carefully to avoid making bubbles. Use the bristle brush to apply the clear varnish coat to the entire Pretty Piggy.

4. Once that coat is dry, lightly sand. Wipe off dust with a damp rag. Repeat this process until at least three coats are applied.

5. Make a loopy bow for the tail. Glue to the hiney. Glue on the eyes. Insert the stopper.

Take note: Pretty Piggy enjoys regular feedings.

MIRROR, MIRROR

Mirror, Mirror, 24" x 30", made by the author

Woo woo, does it get any prettier than this!? You will now have more than your own reflection to admire. "Mirror, mirror, on the wall, who in the land is fairest of all?"*

Materials

Variety of fabric scraps: approximately ½ yard total (.4 pound)
White muslin (optional): ½ yard (.4 pound)

Flowers: 3 pieces of silk: (1) @ 8" x 24"; (1) @ 6½" x 24"; (1) @ 4" x 18"; 3 pieces of organza or netting the same size as the silk; Florist wire (small gauge); Scissors; Buttons

Stem: ¼" cotton cording: 1 yard
Green silk: 1" x 2 yards

Leaves:
Multi-Purpose Cloth (MPC): 12" x 18"
Medium green fabric: 12" x 18"
Light green fabric: 12" x 18"

Buds:
Silk: 5 pieces 3" x 4" in colors that match or complement the flowers
Heavy-duty thread

Other things:
- Framed mirror
- Sponge brush
- Mod Podge
- Small bowl
- MinWax (polycrylic matt finish)
- Inexpensive bristle brush
- Sponge sanding block
- Fabri-Tac

Mirror

1. Remove the mirror from the frame. Lightly sand the entire frame and wipe it with a damp cloth to remove dust.

2. Optional, but preferred, is to cover the frame with white muslin before applying the fabric scraps. To cover it with muslin, measure the width and length of the framing strips and cut muslin pieces that size. In a small bowl, slightly dilute the Mod Podge with a small amount of water so it allows the glue to penetrate the fabric easily. Use the sponge brush to apply a coat of Mod Podge to the frame. Then apply the muslin strips until the front and sides of the frame are covered. The rest of the directions are the same whether you use the muslin or not. An alternative is to spray paint the frame white.

3. Select a piece of fabric (scrap). With the sponge brush, apply adhesive (Mod Podge) to the frame over an area slightly larger than the first piece of fabric. Place the fabric over the adhesive and then paint more on top of the fabric. Be sure to smooth the fabric so no wrinkles remain.

*Quote from http://en.wikipedia.org/wiki/Snow_White

4. Apply more adhesive to an area slightly larger than your second piece of fabric. Then add the second piece of fabric, overlapping the edge of the first piece. Paint more Mod Podge on top of the fabric (figure 1).

5. Continue adding fabric pieces in this manner until the entire frame (front and sides) is covered with fabric (figure 2). Do not worry if you miss some spots. It is much easier to see these omissions after the fabric/ glue has dried. Simply apply more glue and fabric to any spots you missed.

6. After the frame is totally covered and dry, lightly sand it with the sanding block. Remove all the dust with a damp cloth. Carefully stir the MinWax (varnish), avoiding making bubbles. Apply a coat of varnish using the bristle brush. Let dry. Again, sand and then remove dust. Repeat adding coats of varnish at least two more times, sanding between layers. Set the frame aside.

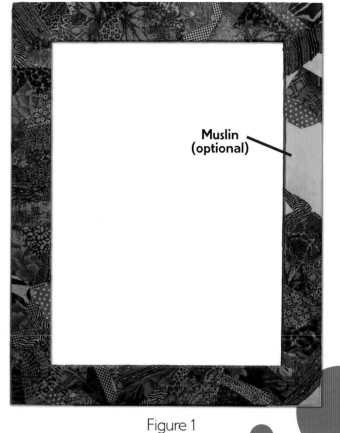

Muslin (optional)

Figure 1

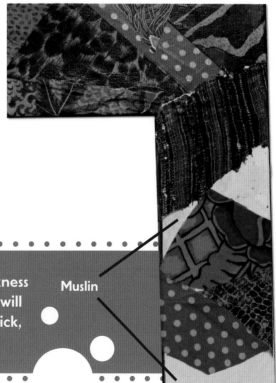

Muslin

Figure 2

Note: Be careful about adding too much thickness to the inside edges of the frame or the mirror will not fit back into its groove. If it does get too thick, take an Exacto knife and remove the excess.

Flowers

1. Lay the 8" piece of organza on top of the 8" piece of silk (figure 3). Pinch the two together at the middle of the 8" side and gather with your fingers (figures 4, 5, and 6).

2. Take a piece of florist wire or heavy-duty thread and twist it in the middle where the flower is gathered (figure 7). Carefully pull the organza layer up to separate from the silk layer (figure 8).

3. Use Fabri-Tac to bond a button to the middle of the flower (figure 9).

4. Repeat these steps for the two remaining flowers. Set aside.

Figure 3

Figure 4

Figure 5

Figure 6

Figure 7

Figure 8

Figure 9

Leaves

1. Using the slightly diluted Mod Podge, coat one side of the MPC. Place one of the 12" x 18" green fabrics onto the MPC cloth. Coat the fabrics on that side with more Mod Podge. Let dry (figure 10).

2. Bond the second green fabric to the other side of the MPC in the same manner. Let dry. Your MPC will now have two contrasting sides.

3. Trace the smaller leaf pattern and the larger leaf pattern on page 74 onto the laminated MPC. Repeat for the number of leaves you use in your design. See the photo of the finished mirror for suggestions.

4. Cut out the leaves. With each smaller leaf, overlap the split end and glue. This makes the leaves three-dimensional. The larger leaves will be used to wrap around the buds. Trim one side of the overlap (figure 11).

Stem

1. Glue one end of the 1" strip of fabric to the end of the cording. Wrap the fabric diagonally around the cording, overlapping the edges (figure 12). Add a dab of glue from time to time to hold the fabric in place.

2. Continue until you have covered enough cording for your stems/vines (figure 13). Glue the end of the fabric to the cording.

Figure 10

Trim one side

Figure 11

Figure 12

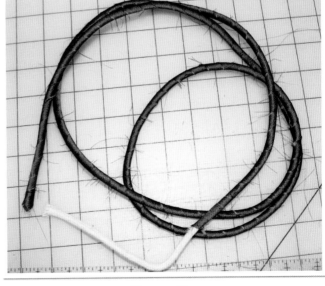

Figure 13

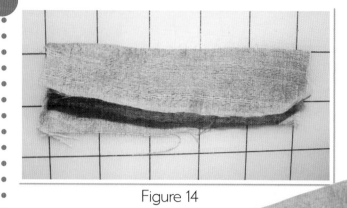

Buds

1. Fold one of the 3" x 4" pieces of silk lengthwise (figure 14). Fold the outer corners down and glue in place (figure 15).

2. With your fingers at the bottom edge (raw edge), roll and slightly gather the fabric (figure 16). Glue the ends and secure them by wrapping with a piece of heavy thread. Tie off the base of the bud (figure 17).

3. Apply glue to the base of the bud and wrap with one of the larger leaves. Hold for several minutes until dry. You can also use a clamp to hold the leaf to the bud until it dries.

4. Repeat these steps for the remainder of the buds.

Assembling

1. Position a stem on the frame as desired. Secure it in several places with Fabri-Tac.

2. Arrange the flowers, buds, and leaves, gluing each in place. If too much glue shows somewhere, add a leaf to cover it.

Very fair, indeed!

Figure 14

Figure 15

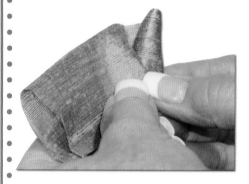

Figure 16   Figure 17

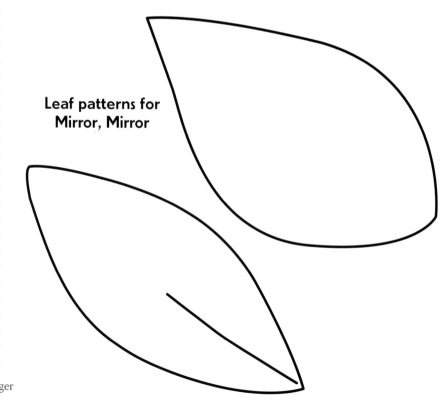

Leaf patterns for Mirror, Mirror

GALLERY

Resources
for a Few of My Favorite Things
(in no particular order)

- Quarter Square (7" tall) by Nifty Notions ("Cut for the Cure"). Look for this line of rulers by Kaye England at your favorite quilt shop.

- Bamboo Batting and Quilter's 80/20™ by Fairfield, www.poly-fil.com (800-243-0989)

- Tom, aka Mr. Wonderful (He's on my speed dial.)

- Steam-A-Seam 2®, The Warm Company, www.warmcompany.com (800-234-WARM)

- Wonder-Under®, Freudenberg Nonwovens, PCP Group, LLC, www.pellonideas.com (727-388-7171)

- Grabaroos® Gloves http://grabaroos.com (877-310-GRAB)

- Quiltsmart® www.quiltsmart.com or info@quiltsmart.com (952-368-3000)

- Roc-lon® Multi-Purpose Cloth™ (US patent 5,741,582, filed September 8, 1995, and issued April 21, 1998) and Roc-lon Permanent Press Muslin from Rockland Industries. Call 1-800-876-2566 to find out which local stores in your area carry Roc-lon products.

- Tom (He knows where I live.)

- Supreme Free-Motion Slider™ by Pat LaPierre, La Pierre Studios, LLC, www.freemotionslider. com or LaPierreStudio@gmail.com

- Tuscany Silk Batting by Hobbs, www.hobbsbondedfibers.com or sales@ hobbsbondedfibers.com Call 1-800-433-3357 if you cannot find the Hobbs product you want at your local retailer.

- Fabri-Tac™ by Beacon Adhesives, www.beaconcreates.com

- Mod Podge®, Plaid Enterprises, Inc., www.PlaidOnline.com (800-842-4197)

- Heat 'n' Bond® Ultrahold by Therm O Web, www.thermowebonline.com

- Tom (He is Mr. Wonderful.)

dianne on dianne

In the last century, when I was about 11 or 12, I remember my older brother saying after a morning of ripping open Christmas gifts, "You know, it just would not be Christmas if Dianne did not get some kind of art project."

The die was apparently cast even before that. I was already hooked on arts and creating things by age 12: paint-by-number; knitting; sewing/designing clothes; drawing; wrapping bottles (and anything else that got in my line of vision) in twine. In other words, I explored all the usual and some not-so-usual creative outlets for a young person.

Move forward into the current century and add dabbling in just about every conceivable form of art or craft to my repertoire. In the process of becoming, I also became one of the oldest living grad students, finally receiving my MFA in 1999. Passing through my heart, hands, and pocketbook were glass beadmaking, glass fusing, batiking, oil painting, watercolor, jewelry design, weaving, garment construction, quilting, kite-making, print-making, enameling, calligraphy, ceramics, sculpture, etc., etc. Should I mention here that I ended up teaching art in the gifted/talented program for 25 years?

Jill-of-All-Trades-Mistress-of-None is my middle name.

At the present time, I have become immersed in the world of quilting. I enjoy anything that involves fabric—from simply fondling the fibers to drawing designs that will become part of those fibers. In 2007 I started a company called, cleverly,

Dianne Springer Designs. Our company, meaning all of my wonderful free helpers and I, create, package, and market products that take the quilt from the bedroom to new and fun places. In 2010 I had the first line of fabrics that I designed become available in the marketplace. And if you're reading this in a book, it means that in 2012 I became an author.

If you are so inclined, please check our website; www.diannespringerdesigns.com.

I would take it as a personal gift if you would also add your name to my BFFs by reading my musings and adding yours to my blog, Threads from My Head, http://diannespringer.blogspot.com.

More AQS Books

This is only a small selection of the books available from the American Quilter's Society. AQS books are known worldwide for timely topics, clear writing, beautiful color photos, and accurate illustrations and patterns. The following books are available from your local bookseller, quilt shop, or public library.

#8523

#8351

#8355

#8529

#8347

#8532

#8528

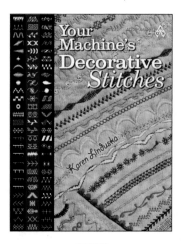

#8353

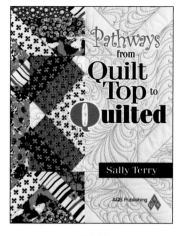

#8348

LOOK for these books nationally.
CALL or **VISIT** our website at

1-800-626-5420
www.AmericanQuilter.com